Llewellyn's
2015
Witches'
Companion

An Almanac for Everyday Living

Llewellyn's 2015 Witches' Companion

ISBN 978-0-7387-2690-8

Art Director: Lynne Menturweck
Cover art © Tim Foley
Cover designer: Lynne Menturweck
Designer: Joanna Willis
Editor: Andrea Neff

Interior illustrations:
Kathleen Edwards: 42, 45, 46, 48, 115, 116, 119, 171, 174, 177, 230, 235
Tim Foley: 9, 64, 66, 70, 85, 99, 103, 105, 135, 147, 193, 194, 197, 219, 240, 242
Bri Hermanson: 53, 54, 57, 59, 88, 93, 94, 150, 155, 158, 257
Jennifer Hewitson: 13, 15, 16, 82, 108, 165, 209, 211, 215, 216, 247, 248, 251
Christa Marquez: 21, 23, 24, 29, 74, 76, 141, 144, 182, 184, 187, 189, 225, 226
Rik Olson: 34, 37, 124, 127, 129, 202, 206, 263, 266, 269

Additional illustrations: Llewellyn Art Department

Any Internet references contained in this work are current at publication time, but the publisher cannot guarantee that a specific location will continue to be maintained.

You can order Llewellyn annuals and books from *New Worlds*, Llewellyn's magazine catalog. To request a free copy of the catalog, call toll-free 1-877-NEW-WRLD, or visit our website at http://www.llewellyn.com.

Llewellyn Worldwide Ltd.
2143 Wooddale Drive
Woodbury, MN 55125-2989
www.llewellyn.com

Printed in the United States of America

Contents

Witchy Living

Day-by-Day Witchcraft

Witchcraft Essentials

Practices, Rituals & Spells

Magical Transformations

Everything Old Is New Again

The Lunar Calendar

September 2014 to December 2015

Community Forum

PROVOCATIVE OPINIONS ON
CONTEMPORARY TOPICS

Embracing the Dark Goddess: Rethinking How We View the Darker Mysteries

Stephanie Woodfield

I have always found comfort in the dark. Whether it was calling on the Goddess under the veiled light of the waning moon or taking solace in the embrace of the wild black-winged Morrigan, and goddesses like her, I have gained strength and become whole through the mysteries of the dark goddess.

She is Kali, adorned in skulls, dancing with abandon. She is regal Hecate guiding Persephone through the darkness of the underworld, and she is the raven goddess Morrigan prophesying upon the battlefield. The dark goddess, in all her many forms, can be a difficult figure to understand. She scares us. She frightens us. She makes us look at hard truths, ones we would rather sweep under the rug and think about later. More often than not, we ignore her mysteries. We forget that there is beauty and power in the dark. Of all the faces of the Goddess, the dark goddess is one we so often shy away from, and is the most misunderstood.

The dark goddess, in all her many forms, can be a difficult figure to understand ... More often than not, we ignore her mysteries. We forget that there is beauty and power in the dark.

So who exactly is the dark goddess? And what does "dark" mean in connection to deity? In general, there are two main misconceptions concerning dark goddesses: first, that they are "evil," and second, that all dark goddesses are guises of the crone.

Both culturally and spiritually, we tend to associate the word "dark" with "evil." Many of us grew up in a spiritual tradition that had very clear concepts of good and evil, and light and dark. This black and white view of the world is difficult to unlearn. Culturally we are taught from a young age that night is when the monsters come out, the bogeyman creeps out from under the bed, and the horror-movie villain emerges. We even use the colors black and white to represent these ideas. We wear black to funerals and when we're in mourning, and view white as the color of purity. The Celts, on the other hand, connected black to fertility, as it was the color of rich fertile soil, while white was connected to death, being the color of bleached bones. As I work primarily with Celtic deities, this is very much how I see spiritual darkness. The dark goddess is that force of nature that destroys in order to create. She breaks down the barriers we create for ourselves and guides us toward change. Like the soil that is made fertile by the decomposition of other life, she forces us to shed what no longer serves us, remaking us anew from the ashes.

Part of why we fear the dark goddess, and mislabel her as evil, is because she represents things we are uncomfortable with. Change frightens us. Sometimes we cling to unhealthy situations because we are afraid that this is as good as it gets. Taking those first steps into the unknown can be terrifying. As much as we say we want change in our lives, we cling with clenched fists to the things we should release and let go of the most. This is the heart of what the dark goddess represents: change and transformation.

For many people, the dark goddess has become synonymous with the crone. More often than not, we connect the term "dark" to "death" (whether physical or symbolic), and therefore relegate them to the realm of the crone. While much of what the crone represents can be considered the realm of the dark goddess, not all dark goddesses are crones. In fact, many of them are maidens and mothers. My own patron, the Morrigan, is often called a triple crone. While at times she appears as a hag, in the vast majority of her mythology she is described as a young, pale-skinned girl or an alluring woman in her childbearing years. Nowhere in the lore does she ever appear as a triple crone, yet the stigma remains that she can only appear as a crone based on the lessons she teaches. Similarly, Hecate, who in modern times is almost always portrayed as a crone, often appeared as a maiden. Several Greek statues show her as a youth in triple form, yet like the Morrigan, we choose to see her only as a crone based on her mysteries.

The dark mysteries are embodied within all the aspects of the Goddess. Ultimately, the dark goddess embodies transformation, whether that be the process of physical death and rebirth or the ending of one

Ultimately, the dark goddess embodies transformation, whether that be the process of physical death and rebirth or the ending of one phase of life and the beginning of a new one. She teaches us that change is a constant process.

phase of life and the beginning of a new one. She teaches us that change is a constant process.

In the guise of the maiden, the dark goddess teaches us to be true to ourselves. As Persephone, she begins as a goddess of spring. When Persephone leaves her mother's side and travels to the realm of spirits, she becomes queen of the underworld. She is a light in the darkness. It is not until she leaves her comfort zone (being with her mother) that she truly comes into her own power. While Persephone dwelled in the underworld, the earth above remained barren, her life-giving energies centered instead within, nourishing the goddess herself instead of the soil and plants.

The Welsh goddess Blodeuwedd is another example of the dark maiden. Blodeuwedd was magically created from flowers to be the husband of the god Llew. When she dared to love another, she was punished by being transformed into an owl, banished to the night for asserting her independence. In Native American mythology, she is the beautiful Sedna, who refused to marry any of the suitors her father picked for her. Angered, her father threw her over the side of his boat, chopping her fingers off as she attempted to climb back in. Her severed limbs transformed into seals and other sea creatures. Again, the dark maiden is punished for her independence, yet through transformation she is reborn in a new form, overcoming the obstacles in her life.

There is no goddess fiercer in the Hindu pantheon than Kali. She wears severed heads and limbs as necklaces and fights demons, yet she is also hailed in traditional prayers as a divine mother, or "Mother Kali." In one story Kali became so lost in bloodlust during battle that she was in danger of destroying all humankind. In one version of the myth, the god Shiva transformed into a baby and threw himself in the raging Kali's path. Once Kali heard the child's cries, her motherly instinct kicked in and she snapped out of her killing rage. Even Gaia, whom we tend to think of as the ultimate mother, was hailed by the Greeks as "All-Fertile, All-Destroying Gaia, Mother of All."[1]

It is doubtful that our ancestors would have seen goddesses who displayed both motherly attributes and a fierce, often warrior nature as being out of the ordinary. We know that in nature there is nothing more dangerous than a mother animal protecting her young. Battle was also a large part of our ancestors' lives. War was not something they observed from afar, as many of us do today. They would have had very real concerns about being invaded by the tribe or country nearest them. Deities of battle were beings of protection; they represented a necessary part of life. Very often these goddesses of battle were also mother figures, their function as battle deities representing their divine protection over the tribe or clan.

Today, we are less comfortable with these concepts. In our culture, motherhood still has a June Cleaver persona. Mothers must be all-loving and all-giving, even to the point of neglecting themselves. The

dark goddess instead represents tough love. She guides us through life but makes us accept the consequences of our choices. She does not coddle us. Like Kali, she can cradle an infant in her arms or take up the weapons of war to defend those she loves.

Ultimately, "dark goddess" is a modern term we use to describe ancient goddesses. While the lessons these goddesses teach require dedication and a willingness both to accept change and to look at ourselves honestly, their mysteries are just as valid today as they were in ancient times. The dark goddess teaches us to dance in the void, to delve into our own darkness and emerge renewed. She is a vital and powerful force, a face of the Goddess we should explore and embrace. Sometimes we fear her, but without her mysteries life could not exist. If nothing changed, if nothing died, there could be no rebirth, no continuation of life. She hands us the cup of truth, allowing us to gaze upon our true selves. She tears us apart, but only so she may lead us to rebirth and renewal. No matter what we have been through in our lives, we can rise from the ashes and, like Kali, dance ecstatically on the ruins of our old selves toward rebirth.

Dark Goddess Spell for Transformation

This is an excellent spell to use to invoke the powers of the dark goddess to bring about change and transformation in our lives. Whether we wish to break a bad habit, find healing, or let go of emotional baggage, the dark goddess can help us overcome the many obstacles life puts in our paths.

You Will Need:
- A black or dark-colored candle
- A pen and paper
- A fireproof bowl

Place the candle representing the dark goddess in the center of your sacred space. On the piece of paper, write down the aspect of your life that you want to transform. Transformation is different than banishment. You will be asking the dark goddess to help you work through this problem or situation and emerge changed. If you ever find that you keep trying to banish the same things magickally, it may be time to rethink your approach and ask for transformation instead. Banishing something is like putting a Band-Aid on a problem: if we don't treat the root cause, then it will continue to appear in our lives.

Sit comfortably. Ground and center. Light the candle, saying:

Lady of change and transformation,
Goddess of the underworld, queen of shades,
Goddess without limitation,

I call upon untamable dark divinity.
Remove all that hinders me.
Teach me how to become whole.
Lady of change, bring transformation in your wake.

Spend a few minutes communing with the dark goddess. See her standing before you. What does she look like? What face does she wear? When you are ready, take the paper and light it with the candle, chanting:

Lady of change, bring transformation in your wake.

Bring the situation or problem you wish to transform to the forefront of your mind. See it clearly. Slowly see the problem transforming into the change you wish to achieve. Ask the dark goddess for her aid in bringing about this transformation.

When you are ready, thank the dark goddess and extinguish the candle. Take the ashes outside and let the wind carry them away.

NOTES

1. Sibylline Order, "Orphic Hymn to Gaia," translated and interpreted by Virginia Stewart-Avalon, M.Ed., http://www.sibyllineorder.org/sacred_texts/oh_gaia.htm.

Stephanie Woodfield *is the author of* Celtic Lore and Spellcraft of the Dark Goddess: Invoking the Morrigan *and* Drawing Down the Sun: Rekindle the Magick of the Solar Goddesses. *Stephanie has been a practicing Witch and Priestess of the Morrigan for over sixteen years. Her articles have appeared in* SageWoman *magazine,* The Portal, *and on the* Witches' Voice *website. She is one of the founding members of* Morrigu's Daughters, *an online sisterhood dedicated to the Morrigan. You can find her on her blog,* Dark Goddess Musings, *at http://darkgoddessmusings.blogspot.com.*

Illustrator: Jennifer Hewitson

Divine Aces: Asexual Gods and Goddesses

Elizabeth Barrette

Mythology often portrays gods and goddesses embroiled in sexual adventures, but not all deities behave that way. Some of them are asexual and/or aromantic. This article explores gods and goddesses who have no interest in carnal or courtship activities.

What is asexuality? In biology, asexuality may refer to life forms that are not differentiated into two sexes, or ones that use alternative reproductive methods such as budding or division instead of combining an egg and a sperm to make offspring. In gender studies, asexuality is a sexual orientation in which a person does not experience erotic desire for other people. Compare this to heterosexuals (who desire members of the opposite sex, but not their own), homosexuals (who desire members of the same sex, but not the opposite), and bisexuals (who desire members of both sexes). Having a category of people that one does not desire sexually is common, and for asexuals, everyone happens to be in that category. Sometimes "asexual" is shortened to "ace."

What is aromanticism? This is an aspect of sexual orientation that deals with forming affectionate partnerships flavored by the activities of courtship that we typically call "romance." Aromantic people are not interested in that type of interaction with anyone. However, they may desire to form other types of connection with friends, coworkers, housemates, and so forth. Sometimes "aromantic" is shortened to "aro."

> **The asexual and aromantic aspects have always been present in humanity and divinity, but they are easily overlooked… So in searching for mythology about asexual and/or aromantic deities, watch for clues like virginity, solitary occupation, asexual reproduction, and rebuffing sexual or romantic advances.**

A majority of people, and therefore many deities who reflect our expectation, are both sexual and romantic. Some are aromantic sexual or romantic asexual. Some are aromantic asexual. All of that diversity is natural and perfectly okay.

The asexual and aromantic aspects have always been present in humanity and divinity, but they are easily overlooked. People tend to focus on the common stuff. Occasionally these aspects of orientation are specified outright, but more often they are shown through actions. So in searching for mythology about asexual and/or aromantic deities, watch for clues like virginity, solitary occupation, asexual reproduction, and rebuffing sexual or romantic advances.

Artemis: Virgin Goddess

Artemis is the Greek goddess of the moon and the hunt. She oversees the wilderness and wild animals. As a virgin goddess, she lives independent of male influence and associates primarily with nymphs, goddesses, and other females. For this reason, she is sometimes interpreted as lesbian. Artemis does not get into sexual or romantic entanglements in mythology. Her sexuality is reserved, inviolable, so it may be reserved for herself alone. She has relationships with others, but they are based on camaraderie rather than romance.

Her passion is all for the hunt and the wild. In this regard, Artemis shows that asexual and/or aromantic people need not be lackluster; they simply wax passionate about different things than sexual people do. So Artemis is almost always portrayed with her bow and arrows, dressed for the hunt, and frequently in the company of forest animals such as deer. The crescent moon, another of her symbols, equates to her bow and likewise appears in many icons of Artemis.

This goddess makes a good patron for people interested in outdoor activities, especially hunting, or environmental issues. Artemis is particularly supportive of young women, although she has male devotees as well. She provides a role model for those of ambiguous sexuality, who may still be questioning their feelings or identity. This is particularly relevant to people who don't feel compelled to jump into a sexual or romantic relationship, but prefer to associate with a group instead.

Athena: Aromantic Asexual

Athena is the Greek goddess of wisdom and war. She is unusual in having an asexual birth as well as orientation. Zeus swallowed the nymph Metis while she was pregnant with Athena, and later Athena sprang out of Zeus's head already full-grown and armored. The myths of Athena firmly establish her as uninterested in romantic or sexual relations of any kind.

Instead, Athena focuses on intellectual and physical pursuits. She gathers and teaches knowledge. She inspires warriors in battle, especially military leaders, granting victory to her chosen followers. She enjoys athletic competitions and the power of her own body. Her civic interest shows in her patronage of the city Athens, which she won by creating the first olive tree. Her connection to war and knowledge shows in her appearance: Athena is always armed and armored, with an aegis shield showing a gorgon head. Often the owl of wisdom appears with her.

Female scholars and warriors count among Athena's favorite devotees, although she accepts men as well. Many famous generals of Greece attributed their success to her patronage. She empowers people to live an independent life without close entanglements of any kind. If that's your goal, consider Athena as a possible goddess for you.

Atum: Aromantic Asexual

Atum is the creator deity in Egyptian cosmology, referred to in early liturgy as "that great He-She." Hermaphroditic deities are often sexualized as the "everymate" capable of attracting and satisfying anyone. This one is neither romantic nor sexual. Atum created Tefnut and Shu, the first male and female, by masturbating. So here we have an asexual deity reproducing asexually. Atum is also described as beyond gender, or perhaps more precisely, before gender.

Diverse representations of Atum exist. He-She is sometimes masculinized as a man wearing a royal head cloth or the dual white-and-red crown of Upper and Lower Egypt. Atum also appears as a serpent, symbolizing the creative cycle. Snakes represent transformation and feminine power in many Pagan religions. Other times Atum is a mongoose, lion, bull, lizard, or ape—a shapeshifter who can be anything, any sex or gender.

Atum is the deity of self-love. He-She represents satisfaction, sufficiency, and pleasure in a solitary lifestyle. Some asexual people dislike sex. Others love masturbation, but just don't want to involve another person in their sex life—for them, Atum makes a terrific patron. The creator aspect also ties in strongly for asexual and/or aromantic people who are writers, artists, musicians, or other creative folks. Genderqueer, intersexed, transfolk, and other liminal individuals may wish to consider Atum as well.

Avalokitesvara: Asexual

Avalokitesvara appears in different manifestations across Hindu and Buddhist traditions. Originally presenting as male, Avalokitesvara later becomes female, particularly in Chinese lore. Bodhisattvas are customarily considered celibate or asexual, and this one is explicitly asexual. Avalokitesvara is occasionally linked with other mythic figures, so a romantic connection is not impossible but is unlikely.

Avalokitesvara has thirty-three manifestations, so there are many symbols and other features available. Among the most common are a white robe, a willow branch, and a white vase holding the "dew of compassion," which can purify the mind and body. Others include a

lotus leaf, a fish basket, a clam, and the moon. Notice the repetition of cleansing and purity.

This bodhisattva deals in compassion and enlightenment and is an excellent guide for followers interested in meditation and personal growth. Male-to-female transsexuals may also appreciate a divine patron who has made a similar journey. Here, too, is an expression of asexuality as a spiritual state of wholeness and purity.

Baron Samedi: Romantic Asexual

Baron Samedi is a loa of death in the Haitian tradition. Loas are spirits who oversee a particular sphere of influence; they can appear in many different variations and blur into each other. Because death and life are so closely linked, the "ghedes," or death spirits, often have a strong sexual component. Baron Samedi is one who can manifest without that. Instead, he represents the gentle and patient side; he is Gentleman Death.

This shows in his appearance. Baron Samedi customarily wears a tuxedo and top hat. He may carry flowers and an ornate walking stick. He wears a monocle or dark glasses, indicating his ability to see the spirit world. Sometimes he appears driving a coach or carriage, a symbol of death as travel.

Baron Samedi is a suave and sophisticated loa. He can teach the mysteries of death to those who wish to learn. He understands the value of courtship, respect, and finesse. This makes him a good guide for people whose jobs relate to death or transportation, but also for those who need strong people skills. He can help develop an appreciation of romance for its own sake, without rushing ahead to the sex.

Khaos: Aromantic Asexual

Khaos is the Greek deity of disorder, sometimes described as a god and other times as a goddess. S/he represents nothingness, the primordial Void from which all of creation emerged. Khaos is also a deity of air and fate. Although asexual, s/he produced children (including Erebus, Eros, Gaia, Nyx, and Tartarus) without needing a partner.

It is difficult to represent the Void with any kind of iconography, so Khaos rarely appears in sacred art. A swirl of clouds or an amorphous starfire would do for an altar object.

Khaos calls to those who are neither one thing nor another, or a little bit of this and that—the undifferentiated ones. This is a good choice of patron for intersexed or genderqueer people. Solitary aromantic asexuals may find this deity appealing, but so may those who wish to raise a child on their own. Practitioners who dislike fancy trappings or elaborate rituals may dispense with those and simply worship the source of All That Is.

Ghede: Aromantic Sexual

Ghede is a loa of death in the Haitian tradition. He lends his name to the whole family of death spirits, called ghedes. Ghede and his kindred spirits tend to be raunchy, lecherous party animals. He considers it a grand joke to possess the most upright person in a congregation and make them do outrageous things. Ghede represents the image of death as an uninvited guest, an interloper, an interruption—but he also embodies the intimate entanglement of life and death. He avoids the social mores of romance and marriage, instead carousing free of obligations. In this way Ghede also fulfills one of the Trickster roles, preventing stagnation.

Like Baron Samedi, Ghede sometimes dresses up, but his suit is as likely to be purple as black and white. It's more poking fun at society than being genuinely respectable. Ghede emphasizes dichotomy: he may paint his face half-white, wear a skull mask, or wear sunglasses with one lens missing. This symbolizes his reign over life and death, the mortal and spirit worlds. Ghede also embodies vices such as smoking, drinking, swearing, and vulgar behavior.

Ghede makes a good guide for people who feel trapped by social expectations. He can break through barriers very effectively—and roughly, so he's not a loa for the faint of heart. Ghede celebrates the physical, the carnal, the reality under the euphemisms. He brings forth the true self in his devotees. He helps people discover the joy of sex and the mastery of their own bodies. He can also get you into a lot of trouble, so be cautious when working with him.

Hestia: Aromantic Asexual

Hestia is the Greek goddess of hearth and home. She deals not in sexual love but in nonsexual love and family ties. As an epichthonic deity, she acts primarily in the mortal realm rather than above it (as with Olympian deities) or below it (chthonic deities). Dwelling in the house, she mediates between above and below, private and public, individual and collective concerns. Hestia represents permanence, security, and continuity.

The symbolism of Hestia is very simple. Often she is represented with just a flame or fireplace. Her public hearth in a city has a plain wooden throne with a white woolen cushion. On rare occasion she appears as a veiled woman with a staff in her hand. Her sacrificial animal is the pig.

Hestia makes an ideal goddess for people who want family as a collective rather than an individual experience. An aromantic-asexual person can belong to an extended family, enjoy the company of others, help raise children as they come along, care for elders, keep up a home—all without needing a bed partner. Then, there is always someone who is not directly caught up in the delights and tensions of romance and procreation, so has extra energy to deal with whatever comes along, a stable centerpiece. Hestia is the hearthstone on which such social infrastructure is built, and she can guide the development with grace.

Kali: Aromantic Sexual

Kali is a Hindu goddess of death, sex, violence, and motherly love. It's a weird combination, but it works for her. She represents the all-consuming march of time. She is destruction, but also creation. She grants enlightenment by obliterating the ego. In her aspect of ferocious mother, Kali stands for reproductive freedom and for the protection of her offspring.

You can see these aspects in her iconography. Kali usually appears with weapons in her many hands. She wears a necklace of skulls or a girdle of severed heads. Often she is dancing. Sometimes she appears having sex with Shiva (who may or may not be decapitated). She may be nude or wearing bloody robes. Her tongue sticks out in a salacious gesture.

People often focus on the violent aspect of Kali. This goddess is a good patron for female warriors or survivors of abuse. However, her aspect as an aromantic sexual and a fierce protector makes her ideal for single mothers, especially those who planned their parenthood and never wanted a coparent. She teaches that you don't need romance to have a child, that it's okay to take a temporary mate and raise the baby yourself. You can be aromantic and still reproduce happily. In her aspect as time, Kali appeals to recordkeepers, historians, archaeologists, and other people who work with or against entropy—especially if they are married to their work.

White Buffalo Calf Woman: Aromantic Asexual

White Buffalo Calf Woman, or Ptesanwi, appears in Lakota tradition. Long ago she came to the people and brought them sacred ceremonies, including the chanunpa, or peace pipe. One of the two hunters who first saw her was consumed by lust. The other told him to leave her alone, because she was obviously a holy person. The lustful hunter did not heed the warning and made unwanted advances. So she wrapped him in her robe and destroyed him.

White Buffalo Calf Woman bears symbols of many sacred things. In human form she typically appears as a beautiful maiden with a

peace pipe, eagle feathers, and a woman's white deerskin dress with lavish decorations. However, as her name suggests, she can also appear as a white buffalo, usually a calf but sometimes a cow. In the myth, her fur turned the four sacred colors: white, yellow, red, and black.

This goddess is like a nun. White Buffalo Calf Woman does not involve herself in romance or sex because she is a holy person. She represents purity and spiritual power. She is also impregnable and capable of protecting herself against threats. She teaches people to live in harmony with nature. This is a good choice of patron for those wishing to follow a spiritual path and avoid intimate relations with others, but who may still feel a close bond with a community and/or the Earth.

Elizabeth Barrette *has been involved with the Pagan community for more than twenty-three years. She served as managing editor of PanGaia for eight years and dean of studies at the Grey School of Wizardry for four years. Her book* Composing Magic: How to Create Magical Spells, Rituals, Blessings, Chants, and Prayers *explains how to combine writing and spirituality. She enjoys magical crafts, historical religions, and gardening for wildlife. Visit her blog,* The Wordsmith's Forge *(http:// ysabetwordsmith.livejournal.com), or her website,* PenUltimate Productions *(http://penultimateproductions.weebly.com).*

Illustrator: Christa Marquez

A Comparative Look at Eclectic Wicca versus Traditional Wicca

Raven Digitalis

The highly eclectic version of Wicca, which is by far the most prevalent in the United States today, differs greatly from the original roots of Gardnerian Witchcraft. For better or worse, the majority of modern Wiccans are no longer "traditional," and do not tend to be focused on initiatory lineage.

Contrary to Wiccan beliefs that were held for a number of recent centuries, Wicca is not an ancient religion. No proof has been produced of any ancient underground Witch cults or secretive Goddess worshipers. Instead, it seems that the majority of individuals across Western Europe did in fact convert to Christian monotheism while still retaining folk traditions and observations in varying degrees of faithfulness. Many of the charms and spells we term "Witchcraft" now were commonplace back in the day, with many of them being practiced by Christians as well as the hunters of alleged Witches themselves.

. . . .

When Gerald Gardner created Wicca in the early 1950s, he drew upon many Celtic charms, superstitions, and Pagan rituals, and a variety of ancient folk traditions. This occurred after he was allegedly initiated into Witchcraft by a woman called Dorothy Clutterbuck, though the only indication of this Indian-born, English-Christian woman's involvement with occultism comes from Gardner's own claims.

Through his creation of Wicca, Gardner was not reviving a preexisting tradition, as he and anthropologist Margaret Murray (and numerous others) proposed. He was instead adhering elements of various practices into one cohesive and successful unit of practice.

Through his creation of Wicca, Gardner was not reviving a preexisting tradition ... There is simply no such thing as the "Old Religion," and family traditions of Witchcraft ("famtrads") have not been proven to exist before the 1950s.

There is simply no such thing as the "Old Religion," and family traditions of Witchcraft ("famtrads") have not been proven to exist before the 1950s. This academic fact is now becoming widely accepted by a number of Wiccan practitioners, whether traditional or eclectic.

Gardner and colleagues drew upon traditions such as Freemasonry, the Golden Dawn, Thelema, Celtic Paganism, and even ancient magickal grimoires. Gardner's work was greatly influenced by interactions with his poetic Priestess Doreen Valiente and England's famed occultist Aleister Crowley. Regardless of Wicca's recent developments, many of the true Old Ways of European Pagan polytheism and folk magick are indeed alive and well today due in part to Gerald Gardner's contributions and in part to the upholding of folk practices within various European family lineages.

. . . .

It's common in *initiatory* Wicca to have what's called a "downline" of initiates if one is a High Priest/ess who utilizes serious occult training and duly initiates others into the Craft. The initiatory line that can be traced back *from* a person is called their "upline," and this is used in Wicca to trace one's lineage back to Gerald Gardner. Some initiates refer to this as "authentic" Wicca, discounting the eclectic movements that are rooted in self-dedication into Witchcraft. However, the majority of lineage-based Wiccans simply view self-dedicated eclectic Craft as *different* rather than invalid.

Does an initiatory downline constitute greater authority or validity in one's Craft? I would argue that it most certainly does not, but it has its place and is an admirable system of both recordkeeping and knowledge preservation, much of which is lacking in eclectic or less-disciplined styles of modern Wicca. Many nontraditional and traditional Witches tend to believe similarly. There are pros and cons to every approach of magick; nothing is "right" or "wrong," but is simply different, and this diversity allows for a beautiful array of human experience and spiritual connection.

Wicca has never been an exclusive spiritual path or religion. Practitioners are encouraged to find their own identity and individual spiritual callings; this is perhaps exemplified by the line *Do as ye will* from the poetic piece now commonly known as the Wiccan Rede.

This line seems to have been lifted (or borrowed) from Aleister Crowley's Thelemic axiom *Do what thou Wilt shall be the whole of the Law*. In this definition, however, *will* refers to a person's True Will, or spiritual destiny. Taking Crowley's definition into consideration, this line of the Rede actually encourages Wiccans to discover, follow, and align to their unique spiritual callings. Both eclectic Wiccans and orthodox British Traditionalists can and should explore a variety of spiritual practices to determine their place within.

· · · · · · · · · · · ·

Some traditional tools of Gardnerian Wicca seem to have fallen out of favor with many American eclectics. The scourge, for example, is a whip or a cat o' nine tails that was originally used in Gardnerian initiations to symbolize the equal-opposite harshness to its compassionate counterpart, "the kiss."

Most sexual unions in a magickal setting, called a Great Rite, are symbolically acted with a cup and an athame, unless a couple is previously committed. This tends to hold true for traditional Wiccans and eclectic Witches. Additionally, modern Wicca does not tend to value strictly heterosexual relations over same-sex coupling when it comes to sexual magick or to relationships in general. Most modern Wiccans also tend to agree that ritual nudity (skyclad practice) has its time and place, but that most public ceremonies do not require it. (It's interesting to note that Gerald Gardner was a devoted naturist, or nudist, which may explain his comfort level with being naked in one's rites.)

Speaking of tools, the athame, or dagger, was originally intended to be a black-hilted knife, ideally inscribed with symbols that originally appear in MacGregor Mathers's translation of the Renaissance magickal grimoire *The Key of Solomon*. The majority of modern eclectic Witches do not necessarily require their athame to have a black handle nor to be inscribed with specific text.

Gardnerian Craft also makes use of a wide variety of other tools that have greatly fallen out of favor in modern *eclectic* circles, including the cords (cingulum), garter, spear, burin, boline, and stang.

. . . .

Various laws, like the Law of Threefold Return, have also fallen out of favor for a more equalized view of karmic give-and-take. Some individuals, however, believe that a person can only claim Wicca if they follow the Law of Threefold Return in addition to the Wiccan Rede, which was written and subsequently published by Lady Gwen Thompson in the 1960s. Still, some lineage-based initiatory Witches have their own views of karma that differ from Gardner's.

Some Witches and some covens simply use the word "Wicca" as a common point of reference for teachings they offer, even if their lessons are sourced in a variety of philosophies in addition to Gardnerian Witchcraft.

For readers interested in the possible origins of a number of traditional Gardnerian tools, texts, and practices, I highly recommend the book *Wicca Magickal Beginnings* by Sorita d'Este and David Rankine.

. . . .

In original Wicca, a person had to be "made a Witch" or "reborn as a Witch" *by* other Witches rather than simply choosing to dedicate and declare himself or herself a Witch, which is a very common practice in modern Craft.

In the Gardnerian structure, those who are initiated in the First Degree are given the titles of "Priest/ess" and "Witch." Those of the Second Degree are bestowed the names "Witch Queen" (female) or "Magus" (male). Those initiated in the Third Degree can be called "High Priest/ess." Though these initiatory terms may vary with each branch, these lofty titles often go unused by eclectic Wiccans; some standard initiates shy away from some of these titles, even using them in jest. Many eclectic self-dedicated Wiccans don't use any of the aforementioned titles, reserving their use only for those who have been initiated (after all, why should the titles be removed from the structure?). With no disrespect intended toward Gardner, I find the terminology and general language used in his Book of Shadows to be a bit self-aggrandizing. This is likely due in part to his idea of perpetuating the validity of a lost tradition of Witchcraft.

The Gardnerian Book of Shadows is sometimes referred to as *the* Book of Shadows. This original document of modern Witchcraft was strictly intended to be copied by hand (not typed or photocopied), ideally with alterations and additions being made by each initiate.

Some Gardnerian initiates, however, prefer to be more orthodox in their practices, choosing not to alter anything from the original text—including Gardner's fascinating list of "Old Laws" allegedly pertaining to ancient Witchcraft traditions.

The vast majority of traditional Witches agree that sabbats and esbats, as perpetuated in the Book of Shadows, should be somewhat altered each time they are performed, thusly adapting rituals to the needs of the local community and to the psychic intuition of the hosts. By the same token, a common traditionalistic view is that if a spiritual system has precisely written initiatory rituals in place, practitioners should not deviate from these initiations as they were written by the founder or founders. (We also see this viewpoint expressed in Freemasonry and other esoteric fraternities like the Golden Dawn.) This ensures that the *egregore*, or astral imprint, of the ritual is energetically reinforced with every initiation. At present, some magickal traditions, such as the American tradition of Georgian Witchcraft, founded by George Patterson and Zanoni Silverknife, have fractured into separate initiatory camps due to variations in initiatory structure and training.

· · · · · · · · · · · ·

Many practitioners who observe Wiccan holidays do not necessarily observe typical Wiccan beliefs, superstitions, or ritualistic structures, and may instead do away with the title "Wiccan," using instead "Pagan," "Neopagan," or simply "Witch" as self-referential terms. Many modern Witches simply do not follow teachings laid out in

Gardnerian Wicca or other systems of British Traditional Witchcraft, and may follow a different syncretized system of Neopagan spirituality entirely. The majority of modern Witches, namely in the United States, tend to practice Neopagan Witchcraft in a form suitable to their individualistic spiritual journeys, which may or may not include elements of original Wicca.

Neo-Wicca is a term that some modern practitioners have adopted, or that has been given to modern eclectic Wiccans by more traditional Gardnerian or Alexandrian initiates. But do people call themselves Neo-Hindus, Neo-Buddhists, or Neo-Christians? Not quite. Though Wicca has changed and adapted in numerous ways from its original form, I don't believe this is just cause to use any *more* modernized term of recognition, not least because Wicca itself is a Neopagan system. The term Neo*pagan* may be a more appropriate descriptor, because its broad terminology leaves each person's personal practice up to interpretation. There is not one singular Pagan practice, but an array of modern traditions—Wicca's variations included—that draw on much older practices. "Eclectic Wicca" or "eclectic Neopaganism" seem like honest terms that both recognize one's diversity while still paying respect to Gardner's modern roots.

What we now call "Witchcraft" is a magick as old as time itself, even if no Pagan cults or traditions have ever been preserved in their entirety…but why should they be? While I and other Witches may take issue with some of Gardner's approaches and claims, it's good to recognize the man's profound contributions to the world of modern esoteric practice. As with all spiritual paths, Wicca is a living tradition that was meant, from the start, to evolve, take shape, and take flight in the hearts of those yearning for self-empowerment and a deeper connection to Mother Earth by way of the Moon Goddess, the Sun God, the cosmic bodies, and one's own deeper consciousness.

Sources

Crowley, Aleister. *Magick, Book Four: Parts I–IV.* Boston, MA: Weiser, 2004.

d'Este, Sorita, and David Rankine. *Wicca Magickal Beginnings.* London: Avalonia Press, 2008.

Digitalis, Raven. *Shadow Magick Compendium: Exploring Darker Aspects of Magickal Spirituality.* Woodbury, MN: Llewellyn Publications, 2008.

Farrar, Janet and Stewart. *A Witches' Bible: The Complete Witches' Handbook.* Custer, WA: Phoenix Publishing, 1981.

Greer, John Michael. *The New Encyclopedia of the Occult.* St. Paul, MN: Llewellyn Publications, 2003.

———. *Secret Societies and Magical History.* Presentation at PantheaCon in San Jose, CA, 2007.

McNevin, Estha. *Opus Aima Obscuræ.* Tradition materials and lesson notes. Missoula, MT, 2003–present.

Silverknife, Zanoni. *Lessons in Georgian Wicca, 101–104.* Class handouts and lecture notes. Missoula, MT, 1999.

Raven Digitalis (Missoula, MT) *is the author of* Shadow Magick Compendium, Planetary Spells & Rituals, *and* Goth Craft, *all published by Llewellyn. He is a Neopagan Priest and cofounder of an "Eastern Hellenistic" Coven and Order called Opus Aima Obscuræ (OAO), and is a DJ of Gothic and industrial music. Also trained in Georgian Witchcraft and Buddhist philosophy, Raven has been a Witch since 1999, a Priest since 2003, a Freemason since 2012, and an empath all of his life. Raven holds a degree in anthropology from the University of Montana and is also a professional Tarot reader, small-scale farmer, and animal rights advocate. He has appeared on the cover of* newWitch *magazine and* Spellcraft *magazine, and has been featured on various print, radio, and television media outlets, including MTV News. Visit him online at www.raven digitalis.com or www.facebook.com/ravendigitalisauthor.*

Illustrator: Rik Olson

Lessons from the Greenwood: Create a Pagan-Based Summer Day Camp for Children

Monica Crosson

Summer sweeps softly across the foothills of the North Cascades, cloaking the Pacific Northwest in a soft mantle of green. As children exchange schoolyards for backyards and parks, local communities are ready with plenty of recreational activities. One activity that is very popular is "Vacation Bible School." These are highly advertised, Christian-based day camps set up by local churches with plenty of singing, games, and snacks to pull in eager young souls. And with the promise of extra points and the bribe of gummy bears and snow cones, the recruiting process begins!

By day two of one local church's event, we received the call. My nine-year-old daughter found me in the garden and asked, "Mom, can I please go?"

"Go where?" I stood up from the rhubarb too quickly and suddenly found my surroundings spinning.

"Melissa called and said she needs to bring a friend to Bible school tomorrow so they can win the ice cream bars. Mom, there are going to be pony rides! Can I go?"

I tried to control my dizziness and process the information at the same time. "What? Bible school? Chloe, you know how I feel about that."

Her expression faded. "Mom, I promise I won't listen. I just want to ride a pony and get some ice cream with Melissa. Please, Mom."

Reluctantly, I told her no. And from the expression she wore, I felt like I had just relinquished my Mother of the Year award.

"It stinks!" I later commented to a coven mate about the situation.

"Yeah," she agreed. "Wouldn't it be great if there was a Pagan-based day camp around here for the kids?" The idea struck us both at once, and the air became electric with our excitement. We would start our own Pagan-based summer day camp.

The first thing we decided was not to use the camp as a recruiting tool, but to invite only the kids from the relatively large number of Pagan families already living in the area.

The next task was to find a location. I had a friend and coven mate who

> **"Wouldn't it be great if there was a Pagan-based day camp around here for the kids?" The idea struck us both at once, and the air became electric with our excitement. We would start our own Pagan-based summer day camp.**

owned a hundred-acre organic farm on a creek. Perfect. We planned our curriculum. We thought we would do a five-day camp and would use one of the four elements (plus spirit for the fifth) as a theme for each day. With a relatively small amount of cash, a lot of creativity, and some wonderful volunteers, School of the Greenwood was born.

We began on a sultry July afternoon. Sixteen children filed down a path lined by foxglove and perfumed with the heady scent of sweet woodruff. As the children filled out our circle, puffs of cottonwood floated on a lazy breeze. There were giggles of excitement, and then one small girl said, almost in a whisper, "The fairies have come."

"Yes," I agreed, "I believe there are fairies in our midst."

What a magickal first year that was, too! It has been five years since we put together that first day camp, and we have learned so much. So if you have ever wished that there were simple instructions for how to run a Pagan day camp, well, wish no more! This article will give you helpful guidelines to assist you in planning what could be one of the most meaningful, magickal experiences for the children who attend.

Location, Location, Location!

The most difficult part of the planning process can be finding a location big enough to host a day camp that has plenty of outside room to run and play games but also has proper bathroom facilities and an indoor area in case of inclement weather. I'm from Washington State, and the weather can be tricky here. Long-range forecasts are never reliable, especially for those of us who call the foothills our home. Clouds can suck in around the mountains, and a clear day in Seattle can still mean rain for us.

A public park, with permission from the city leaders, can be a good low-cost spot if there is a building where you can bring the children inside. If you live in a rural area, like I do, there may be someone who has property with a structurally sound, covered area that could be used. School of the Greenwood is held on an organic farm that is just a couple of miles from town. We have use not only of a barn for indoor activities but also of a community house that has kitchen and bathroom facilities and room to store our curriculum and art supplies.

Licensing

The majority of states require licenses to run day camps. The fees for the licenses vary from state to state. Some states don't require licenses if the camps last seventy days or less. This is the case for Washington State. The American Camp Association has a great website that allows you to easily find the licensing requirements for your state. Just go to this page: www.acacamps.org/publicpolicy/regulations/print.

States normally require liability insurance coverage for day camps as part of their license requirements. The amount of liability coverage that's legally needed varies by state. The property we use happens to be the site of many community events and was already covered by liability insurance. We just pay a small fee to the farm for our week's coverage.

Along with general liability insurance, you may need coverage for specific adventure-based activities that may be held on the grounds, such as swimming or rock climbing. Auto insurance may also be required if you plan on transporting kids to other locations for activities such as hiking. Check with your insurance company, because many of them offer specific day camp policies that cover the children and the camp staff.

Budget

Keeping to a budget is really important. We have a lot of creative people in my coven who have amazing ideas but also know how to be thrifty. I'm amazed every year at what we are able to offer the children for very little money.

In designing a budget to cover the cost of the day camp, you might want to include site rental, licensing and insurance, salaries (if applicable), curriculum materials and supplies, t-shirts, transportation (if you plan on transporting children), food, and refreshments.

We offer our camp to children free of charge, but if you plan on charging a fee to campers, consider the total cost of your budget and divide that by the number of children your day camp can accommodate to determine the fee you will charge each camper. Try to keep fees as low as possible to allow more children to participate. Another nice idea is to offer scholarships or other reduced fees if more than one child will be attending from the same family.

Staff

Having a fun, supportive, and creative staff to work with is important. Our staff is made up of volunteers. The number of staff members needed will be determined by the number of campers, their ages, and their special needs.

We average about twenty-five campers, and there are typically ten of us on site with the children. Our staff is made up of coven members and our older children (teen or college-age). It is recommended that staff members be at least sixteen years of age.

Depending on your state, staff members may have to go through a background check. If you don't know your volunteers or are hiring staff, it's a good idea to require a background check.

Themes

Come up with a theme for your camp. This is a way for your circle or coven to stretch its creative muscles. Themes can come from anywhere. You can keep it witchy and focus on ideas such as the elements or spellcasting (give it a Harry Potter atmosphere, including a croquet-style game of quidditch). Spend a week in the mystical, dreamy land

of the fey and the ways of fairy magick. We used Shakespeare's *A Midsummer Night's Dream* as our inspiration. World myths is another fun theme. Concentrate on a single myth from a different country each day or a god and goddess from a different culture for each day. Better yet, if you have enough material, you can focus your entire week on the myths and gods/goddesses of one culture. One year we spent the week discovering modern world religions. Our focus that year was tolerance.

We also like to include community service in the camp. Our campers have collected items for the local food bank, packaged seeds to give away at a seed exchange, planted trees along a riparian zone, and made gifts for the residents at a local nursing home.

Schedule

Having a strict plan of action is crucial to creating a camp experience that is enjoyable for both campers and staff. We put together a daily camp schedule weeks in advance, with both rainy and sunny activities penciled in. Even though day camp is all about having fun, structure is necessary to maintain order.

The week before camp, you may want to hold a parent meeting. This is a good opportunity to hand out informational sheets detailing the activities and rules and a plan of action for discipline. Ask for parental support in making their children aware of the camp guidelines before they start, and provide a sign-up sheet for bringing refreshments to an end-of-camp party.

Once you have your plan, clearly communicate each day's schedule to the day camp staff. Your schedule should be well balanced and varied. Include the following areas in your schedule: crafts, recreation, rest and relaxation, and activity times. Above all, remember to be flexible.

A Day in the Greenwood

We like to have our volunteers arrive an hour before the campers. This gives us time to review the schedule and make sure everything is ready to go. Kids get restless if they have to wait for unorganized volunteers to set up a craft table, and restlessness can lead to mischief.

Just before the children arrive, we gather around our circle and ask the Goddess to bless the property and all who gather:

Oh Great Mother,
Bless our path.
Help us to act on your wisdom.
Help us to blessings and lessons so we may pass them on to those we
    teach.
Bless this day.
Keep us safe and whole,
And inspire us so we may face the day with courage,
kindness, insight, and creativity.
So mote it be.

This is when the first smiling faces burst through the garden gate that leads to our circle. After hugs and greetings, it's time to begin. During our opening circle, the kids are presented with our "word of the day," and the talking stick is passed to discuss what it means to them. We close by singing or chanting. Favorites include "Place

of Power," "Goddess with Me," and "Earth My Body."

Circle is followed by a story that is elaborately narrated and acted out by volunteers. We try to pick stories that not only can be identified by our theme, but also spark thought and dialogue among the children. The rest of the day is

Circle is followed by a story that is elaborately narrated and acted out by volunteers ... The rest of the day is spent busily, yet blissfully, rotating between craft tables, greenhouses, and playfields.

spent busily, yet blissfully, rotating between craft tables, greenhouses, and playfields.

You may find us creating poetry masks (a reflection of our inner beauty) or planting magickal herb gardens in small planter boxes constructed and decorated by our campers. We may be on one of the many forested trails on a wild edible scavenger hunt (this one is highly supervised by experts in the field) or creating fairy costumes for an end-of-camp Fairie Ball. No matter what we're up to, it's always a good time.

Plenty of water and fresh fruit and vegetable snacks are provided to the campers throughout the day, but campers bring their own sack lunches. We enjoy our lunches in the shade of an old big-leaf maple, jacketed in moss and hanging with lichen. There is always plenty of play among the kids, and it's wonderful to see how the different age groups interact.

After lunch, it's back to the fun—more stories and songs and plenty of opportunity for artistic expression. We may be making paper for a Book of Shadows or learning about riparian zones on the creek.

As the day comes to an end, we gather back around our circle. We have beads that we use to bestow special blessings on campers who performed an act of kindness. They may have helped a fellow camper in need, cleaned up after a craft project, or simply had a kind word to say. Any volunteer or camper can give out beads during this time. The children construct bracelets, necklaces, or anklets out of them and wear them on the last day. We have never held a camp where there was a child who wasn't completely dangling in beads!

SpiralScouts International

Day camps are great, but the downside is your kids only get to participate in the fun one week per year. If you're looking for something that provides a year-round, family-based scouting experience for your children, you should give SpiralScouts a try.

SpiralScouts originated through the Aquarian Tabernacle Church (ATC) out of Index, Washington, and was created in response to Boy Scouts of America's (BSA's) attitudes and policies about gay people and BSA's lack of background screening of leadership. ATC wanted to provide a scouting experience that Pagan kids would not feel left out of, culturally.

According to their website, "SpiralScouts thrives on child-directed activities based on a globally oriented philosophy of religious tolerance and interfaith cooperation, personal responsibility, and ecological education and conservation, in order to help our children learn to grow into strong, competent members of society."

If you're interested in joining a circle or hearth or starting your own charter, visit their website at www.spiralscouts.org.

Greenwood Reflections

As the last campers make their way back through the garden gate and down the path, I always take a moment to catch my breath. There is a lot involved with running a day camp. After months of planning and preparation and hard work, sometimes I wonder, is it really worth it?

Then I feel a tug at my skirt and see a small red-headed boy wearing a crown of sword fern, with chocolate frosting painting his lips. "Excuse me," he says.

"Yes, Eli," I say, smiling. "What can I do for you?"

"Nothing," he says. "I just wanted to say I had the best time in my whole life." A toothy, jack-o'-lantern grin spreads across his face.

Yes, it is definitely worth it!

Monica Crosson is a Master Gardener who lives in the beautiful Pacific Northwest, happily digging in the dirt and tending her raspberries with her husband, three kids, two goats, two dogs, three cats, a dozen chickens, and Rosetta the donkey. She has been a practicing Witch for twenty years and is a member of Blue Moon Coven. Monica writes fiction for young adults and is the author of Summer Sage. Visit her website at www.monicacrosson.com.

Illustrator: Kathleen Edwards

Ideas, Intellectual Property, and the Age of Plagiarism

Susan Pesznecker

Today, good readers, we're here to talk about plagiarism. It's a somewhat daunting subject, and, given the context, it's only fair I begin by outing myself thoroughly. I'm a published writer, a blogger, a member of a Web-based Druid order with an online apprentice program, a teacher in an online school of magick and arcane arts, and, in my mundane life, a college English and writing professor. In each of these ways, I work every day with the written word. Writing, for me, is a form of artistic expression as well as my livelihood, and I care very much about both sharing and protecting my written works. And that's where plagiarism comes in. It's a deeply personal subject to me because I've found my works used all over the Web without permission and with me—their creator—never acknowledged. I've even found one of my books being sold in e-format on a downloadable torrent site. So yes, this subject matters to me. It should matter to all of us.

Types of Plagiarism

Let's begin with a definition. In the simplest terms, plagiarism occurs when Person A takes or uses Person B's intellectual property (writing, photography, film, music, art, or even ideas) without giving Person B credit. This leaves the reader/viewer/listener assuming the material

is Person A's creation, which it isn't. That's plagiarism, and not only is this rude and unethical, it's actually a form of stealing. The word plagiarism comes from Latin roots meaning "kidnapper" or "a kidnapping," again clearly indicating plagiarism to be a kind of theft.

Plagiarism can be accidental or intentional. The accidental form takes place when Person A doesn't realize she needs to give credit when using someone else's materials or ideas or when she tries to credit the material but does so incorrectly—for example, when she forgets to place quotation marks around exact words. The good news is this kind of accidental plagiarism should only be a temporary issue: it's very easy to learn a simple way of handling and citing source materials (we'll talk about this later in the article), and once a person understands how and why to cite materials and does so consistently, the problem is solved.

Of course, plagiarism can be intentional, too. Person A may believe that by changing a few words or swapping a few synonyms, she's changed the material enough to make it "hers" or perhaps changed it enough that no one will recall the original. Alas, this logic is wrong. When we restate a piece of source material in our own words, we create what's called a paraphrase. But even when paraphrasing, the material's creator still must be acknowledged, because the paraphrase is *still* the other person's intellectual property. Simply changing some words around doesn't alter that essential fact.

In more serious cases of intentional plagiarism, the writer doesn't make an effort to credit the material's creator even though she knows she should. Sometimes this is an act of laziness. In our digital age, it's all too easy to cut and paste material from a Web source, change a few words, and hope no one will notice. Many less-than-ethical people

do exactly this. Or sometimes a writer just doesn't care and tries, intentionally, to portray the stolen material as her own, presumably to make herself look smart, sell a product, or maybe attract a following.

In our digital age, it's all too easy to cut and paste material from a Web source, change a few words, and hope no one will notice. Many less-than-ethical people do exactly this.

Why does this matter? It matters because plagiarism is unethical. It's unfair. It's a form of stealing that deprives people of credit—and sometimes income—for their original creative works. Imagine how you'd feel if you wrote a blog post including your poetry, blessings, photographs, or other works only to find them showing up later on the Web without giving you any credit whatsoever. I know how I felt one morning when I found my book on that BitTorrent website, available to purchase (from someone else!) for download. A Druid friend took the same gut-punch recently when a number of her handwritten charms and prayers appeared in someone else's blog with no mention of her as the author.

Plagiarism. It's just wrong.

I think many people today are confused about information being "free." We're living in the digital information age. I type a question into Google, and two seconds later, half a million answers are at my fingertips. Click any one of those, and in two seconds I'm reading a detailed response. In many ways, this type of information access is near-miraculous, especially to those of us who remember spending days in the library stacks, using ancient card catalogs and worn-down-to-nubs pencils to hunt down a specific dusty journal in hard copy. But instant access comes with its own pit-traps. Just because information is at our cyber-fingertips does not mean it's free for the taking. The owner must be respected and acknowledged...always. Always! And let's mention, while we're at it, that although there's a lot of good material on the Web, there's a great deal of crap, too. Making the matter even more complex, issues such as fair use, copyright, public domain, and Creative Commons are constantly evolving and will continue to do so in our exploding digital age.

Avoiding Plagiarism

For now, let's focus on avoiding plagiarism as the first step in handling information ethically. Here are the simple keys to avoiding plagiarism:

1. First, work from a central ethical position of respect for your work and the work of others.

2. Second, always *do your own work*, relying on your own ideas and inspirations as much as possible. Doing your own work is always the best place to start. After all, if you're trying to create an article or blog entry or book chapter based on your own thoughts and ideas, those ideas are exactly what you should rely on. Your reader wants to know what *you* think and wants to hear about *your* approach; he isn't the least bit interested in how well you can glue together a bunch of other people's source materials to create an opinion or idea that isn't even yours. Plus, if you use only your own ideas, you can't be accused of plagiarizing.

3. Third, if you bring in source materials to add authority or information to your written works, *always* cite the creator of those materials. Apply this rule to any type of intellectual property used: photographs, words, music, film, original ideas, and so forth.

It's just that simple to avoid plagiarism. It truly boils down to those three simple steps.

Giving Credit

In terms of giving credit, there are many ways to do so, depending on how detailed you want to be. But regardless of your approach, the underlying goals are the same. As the user of someone else's intellectual property, you have two key obligations when citing it:

1. First, by citing the source, you give credit to the creator of the material, thereby avoiding plagiarism. This keeps your writing honest and ethical and keeps you in the clear. And let's be clear: the world of "scholarship" allows—even encourages!—us to build off of  one another's work. This is how research happens and how new ideas take shape. But using someone else's work or ideas always requires us to give them proper credit.

2. Second, by describing the material's point of origin as explicitly as you can, you create a paper trail that makes it possible for readers to locate and examine the original source should they wish to. This shows your respect for the material and for your readers.

Part of handling sources is knowing how to manage source material in your own writing. Source material can be quoted, paraphrased, or summarized. When quoting a source, type the exact words into your content, surround the text with quotation marks (signaling the reader that he's reading exact, unchanged language), and follow with an in-text citation (see the Mac Uistin citation in the following example). To paraphrase content from a source, restate the content in your own words but don't use quotation marks. Then add an in-text citation (see the Nowakowski citation in the following example). Do the same for a summary, which is a paraphrase in condensed form.

> Different theories have been proposed as to what Newgrange was and why it was built. Excavations have shown that Ireland's Neolithic sites were focal points or even territorial markers for the surrounding communities (Nowakowski, 43). Their newly honed living skills helped Ireland's Neolithic dwellers to build a thriving permanent community and allowed them to abandon their nomadic ways. Archaeological evidence suggests that the Brú na Bóinne complex was probably the most important cultural center in Europe at the time, with Newgrange being the most important part of the complex. "Neolithic Europe was not a time 'before civilization.' It was, instead, a true civilization in the best sense of the word" (Mac Uistin, 27).

Academic and Professional Styles of Citation

In academia, a number of academic styles are used for source materials. For example, American Psychological Association (APA) style is used by students in the empiric disciplines (science, math, engineering, etc.), while Modern Language Association (MLA) style is used for the humanities (literature, religion, philosophy, etc.). If you know either of these, you can use them in your own works. If working with

a publisher, a specific format may be required. *The Chicago Manual of Style* (CMS) is used by most publishers. Make your best effort to cite the material as completely as you can.

Creating In-Text Citations

An in-text citation is, literally, a citation placed within your written content immediately following each use of source material; this shows the reader exactly where source material has been used and thus shows him which words are *yours* and which come from source material.

Note that putting a citation at the end of a paragraph is unclear: your reader won't know if you're citing only the final sentence, the whole paragraph, or something else. Cite *every sentence* in which source material is used.

The simplest approach to in-text citing is to use a parenthetical citation, which is literally a citation within parentheses. Put a citation at the end of every sentence that uses source material. If you know the author's name, use that: (Smith). Add a page number if available: (Smith, 612). Don't superscript or subscript your in-text citation; superscripts and subscripts don't work with all formats and can ruin your spacing and layout.

Web sources don't have page numbers and may not have author names, either. If your Web content has an author, simply use the author's name as your citation: (Smith). If no author is listed, just use the first one to three words of the article or page title: (Watching the Moon).

Important: Simply providing a URL (Web address) is *not* a sufficient citation. For one thing, our goal is to cite the author and work, not the website. Also, URLs often break or become inactive, leaving the source effectively uncited and setting you (the writer) up for charges of plagiarism.

Creating a List of Sources

After citing your materials within the text of the document, you also need to create a list at the end of the work, listing each source used in the work and thus creating the paper trail mentioned earlier. The following are some models for creating a source list. These examples don't follow any academic style precisely, but they meet the implied requirement of creating complete citations. Note that I've used italic font instead of underlining to show book and periodical titles; this is the current standard in the various types of academic citations.

Books

Last name, first name. *Title*. Publication city: Publisher, Publication date.

Pesznecker, Susan. *Crafting Magick with Pen and Ink*. Woodbury, MN: Llewellyn Publications, 2009.

Web Pages

Last name, first name. "Article/Page Title." *Website Title*. Article or page date. URL.

Green, Heather. "Pagans, Witch Hunts, and the Stand for Human Rights." *The Wild Hunt*. August 24, 2013. wildhunt.org.

Magazines/Periodicals

Last name, first name. "Article Title." *Periodical Title*. Publication date, page numbers.

Moyer, Michael. "Why Does Food Taste So Delicious?" *Scientific American*. September 2013, pp. 26–29.

List your sources in alphabetical order. This makes it easy for the reader to locate items quickly. Here is how I would list the two sources given earlier in the sample paragraph:

Mac Uistin, Liam. *Exploring Newgrange*. Dublin: O'Brien, 1999.

Nowakowski, Jacqueline A. "Neolithic Burial Sites." *British Heritage*. Mar. 1997, 40–47.

By following these guidelines, your article is now carefully cited, and you've handled the materials ethically and avoided any worries over plagiarism. Well done!

Resources for Further Exploration

"APA Formatting and Style Guide." *The Online Writing Laboratory (OWL) at Purdue University.* 2013. http://owl.english.purdue.edu/owl/resource/560/01.

"Chicago Manual of Style 16th Edition." *The Online Writing Laboratory (OWL) at Purdue University.* 2013. http://owl.english.purdue.edu/owl/resource/717/01.

"Defining and Avoiding Plagiarism: The WPA Statement on Best Practices." *Council of Writing Program Administrators.* 2003. http://wpacouncil.org/node/9.

Foster, Star. "Plagiarism, Copyright Infringement, and Piracy." *Patheos.* January 23, 2011. http://www.patheos.com/blogs/pantheon/2011/01/plagiarism-copyright-infringement-and-piracy.

Gabriel, Trip. "Plagiarism Lines Blur for Students in Digital Age." *New York Times.* August 1, 2010. http://www.nytimes.com/2010/08/02/education/02cheat.html?pagewanted=all&_r=0.

"MLA Formatting and Style Guide." *The Online Writing Laboratory (OWL) at Purdue University.* 2013. http://owl.english.purdue.edu/owl/resource/747/01.

Susan Pesznecker *is a writer, college English teacher, and hearth Pagan/Druid living in northwestern Oregon. Her magickal roots include Pictish Scot and eastern European/Native American medicine traditions. Sue holds a master's degree in nonfiction writing and loves to read, stargaze, camp with her wonder poodle, and play in her biodynamic garden. She's co-founder of the Druid Grove of Two Coasts and teaches nature studies and herbalism in the online Grey School. Sue has authored* Crafting Magick with Pen and Ink *(Llewellyn, 2009) and* The Magickal Retreat *(Llewellyn, 2012) and regularly contributes to the Llewellyn annuals. Visit her at www.susan pesznecker.com and www.facebook.com/SusanMoonwriterPesznecker.*

Illustrator: Bri Hermanson

What's in a Degree?

Charlynn Walls

It was not too many years ago that I began the search for my own personal truth: my path to a meaningful spiritual practice. As many Wiccans and Pagans I know have done, I began my journey on my own. I started by doing serious research on my chosen path. I collected books and periodicals and amassed a wealth of information on various aspects and traditions of Wicca and Paganism.

What I came to appreciate and understand over the years was that I was being given a chance to define not only my path but myself as well. I was able

to take the time to mull over the items I read and internalize them. When I could not find others to show me the way, I started writing and doing ritual on my own. I found what worked for me and what did not. I was not burdened by being told what was or was not the proper way to do something.

When I began to be comfortable within my own skin, I started reaching out to those within my local community. I wanted to work with others and expand my knowledge beyond what I could learn on my own. I started getting involved with local groups, both those open to the general public and those that only held closed rituals. Each group I belonged to had their own structure in place. Now, many Wiccans and Pagans may debate the necessity of structure, but every group has one. Even the choice to have an absence of formalized rules is a structure of sorts.

In my area of Missouri, the "Show-Me" state, the people I first interacted with valued knowledge of the Craft, but they were not overly concerned with how that knowledge was gained. There was no stigma attached if you had not studied a formal tradition and obtained a degree. The interactions simply had value based on the competency of the individual. In fact, there were many groups that did not want to train or work with anyone unless the person was first an accomplished solitary practitioner.

For those who have decided to work with a coven or circle, there are numerous variations on formalized traditions and there are those that follow eclectic pathways. However, there are generally two types of groups: non-degree-based systems and degree-based systems.

Non-Degree-Based Systems

Over the years, I have been involved in a coven and a circle that chose not to have any degrees associated with their practice. These groups have had a laidback and easygoing feel to them. They were great for honing magickal interactions within a group setting, and getting a feel for how energy works between individuals and how to harness it. The expectations of the coven were just as relaxed as the rest of the atmosphere.

STRUCTURE

In groups that follow a non-degree-based system, each person is on equal footing with the other individuals within the group. Each person shares in the duties and tasks needed to run the coven, including leadership roles. The individual is considered a priest/priestess of the divine and is capable of leading the rites within that coven or circle. There are no assigned roles, and everyone is encouraged to actively participate. There is a sense of camaraderie and family that surrounds these groups, since everyone leans on one another in order to make the coven function.

There is a downside to this type of structure. A sense of complacency can develop from this type of interaction. People are creatures of habit, and if we are not challenged, we typically stick to what we consider safe. Sometimes we find a role we are comfortable filling, and that's what we stick with in a non-degree-seeking atmosphere.

The group that I worked with held an initiation ceremony for those coming into the group to make their transition official. We assumed the duties necessary to fulfill the needed roles for the Sabbats and Esbats we participated in, but there was rarely a time when we moved beyond our comfort zones. There were many times when the same people assumed the roles of priest or priestess or took a favorite quarter to call.

EDUCATION

Learning practices and pace in a non-degree-based system are determined by the individual. In some instances, the group will discuss a topic of interest to the group, but there are no formal learning requirements. If the individual is motivated, they pursue individual interests on their own time. There are no time limitations or deadlines to meet within this system. While this gives a great deal of freedom to the practitioner, it also leaves them open to the possibility of stagnation in their studies.

When the individual is trying to figure out what course of study to tackle next, it can be overwhelming and the student cannot decide. They stall out and no longer push themselves to continue learning at all. It can create a problem within the group by breeding resentment between the members who want to learn and those who are content with the status quo. That happened in one group that I worked with. We had all been part of a study group prior to accepting initiation into the coven. There were several members who wanted to continue to learn in a similar manner together, but the coven as a whole did not support that kind of learning environment. The relationships between individuals within the group became strained due to the frustration caused by the lack of structured learning.

Practice

The individuals in the non-degree-based system have a more personal practice even though they are practicing as a group. There is an enormous emphasis placed on personal responsibility in this type of system. The individual is responsible for learning what is important and translating that into what is in the best interest of the group.

There is, unfortunately, a chance that not all the members of the coven will agree on what is the best way to practice their craft together. Though this type of system can be more democratic, it can also lead individuals to feel that their beliefs and

The individuals in the non-degree-based system have a more personal practice even though they are practicing as a group. There is an enormous emphasis placed on personal responsibility in this type of system.

ideas are being disregarded. They may not be as vocal as others in the group and may feel overshadowed because their ideas are not heard as often.

Degree-Based Systems

During my courses of study, I have also been fortunate to work with a couple of different traditions that have degree-based systems. These groups have been slightly more formal and have had a greater amount of focus. There were specific expectations and goals that were clearly outlined from the beginning. In these groups, you know what you need to learn in order to progress to the next level.

STRUCTURE

There are various degree systems in place throughout Wicca. The most common is a three-tiered degree system. Each stage in the process is marked with studies that must be completed and often include a minimum time requirement. The mentors and elders of the group will ultimately determine the readiness of the candidate before any degree is bestowed upon the person.

The seeker comes to the coven and is deemed a dedicant of the group. The dedicant and the coven work toward a possible partnership during a courtship period that typically lasts for a year and a day. At that point, if the person has completed the prerequisite studies to a level of satisfaction that the coven is comfortable with and if the person is a good fit, they will be offered First Degree status. A First Degree initiate should be comfortable taking on any role within the group's rituals/rites and will be competent in the basics of Wicca. They will then have a list of requirements that must be met to move on to the next rank. When they have accomplished those tasks, the Second Degree will be conferred. Typically, individuals at this degree are considered to be able to teach the Craft due to their level of expertise. The Second Degree initiates will then have another set of lessons and projects that will continue to challenge them in order to prepare for the Third Degree. The Third Degree initiate is a person who should be able to lead and run a group of their own in the future.

Education

In a degree-based system, there is a great deal of emphasis placed on structured learning. There are clearly outlined standards and goals that you have to meet in order to move from one degree to the next. Often, there are tests or practical applications that have to be completed or observed as a part of the outlined curriculum.

Many of these groups use a mentorship system to help the practitioner move through this process. The mentor acts as a guide to the person who is seeking the degree. They offer insights and practical advice. They can even act as a sounding board if the student is having trouble with a lesson or activity that the coven has deemed necessary. This helps create another bond and level of kinship within the group.

Practice

The degree-based system honors the mystery tradition within Wicca where the initiated are allowed participation in the secret rites and are privy to the information of the tradition. The mysteries of each tradition may be slightly different based on the knowledge that they feel is important to bestow upon you. Each stage is marked by initiation in order to give the practitioner the ability to experience the mysteries. It is a rite of passage marking your achievement within your group. These are aspects that are being pushed more and more to the wayside, but which can have a significant and powerful impact upon the initiate.

There are several pitfalls of this system, including the bureaucratic red tape that comes with conferring degrees. People can become consumed with the "right way" to complete a task, when there may be more than one way to achieve the same goal. There are also individuals and groups who feel that being part of a hierarchical system is the only way to become a "real Witch." They seek out the degree as validation of their spirituality. There are others who see it as a boost to their ego and feel that people will automatically defer to them if they say they are a "Third Degree." I have personally seen people who come into a new community and the first thing they put out is what degree they hold. In my area, we respect that it probably took a great deal of time to achieve that goal. However, most of the people I know are the type who will give you more credence and acceptance if you show them that you are competent instead of insisting that you are.

Conclusions

Since I have been on both sides of the fence in regard to non-degree-based and degree-based groups, I have had the opportunity to weigh the pros and cons of each. There is a lot to be said about a relaxed group of friends/family coming together to mingle energy and practice their magickal craft. The group of people who choose this route really need to be cognizant of the pitfalls. They should be bound together as a family unit and treat the coven as extended family. This really makes the challenges easier to deal with. It also creates a different mindset that allows for more open communication.

The degree-based groups tend to be more organized in regard to continuing education. They also seem less prone to stagnation, since the members of the coven are moving forward toward pre-set goals. The individuals strive to continue learning along their chosen path, which involves the entire group through leadership and mentoring roles. The mysteries also play a pivotal role to the initiate. The initiatory system provides a rite of passage based on the acknowledgment of achieved knowledge and proficiency in the Craft. The rite allows initiates to experience the lessons they have learned, thus changing them in profound ways.

. . . .

You really have to know your group of individuals and their needs in order to make an educated decision on which type of group to create. Also, it is important to be aware of the expectations of an established group that you may be looking to become a part of, because you want to make sure that they will be able to meet your needs both in and out of ritual. The best groups work well on multiple levels, and their members check their egos at the door, considering what is best for the group.

Charlynn Walls *has written articles for Llewellyn's annuals and conducted interviews for* Witches & Pagans *magazine. She possesses a BA in Anthropology with an emphasis on Archaeology. She has been a guest on several radio programs discussing both spiritual issues and the impact of archaeological finds on modern Paganism. Charlynn also works with Witch School International. As an educator and leader in the Pagan community, she is well into a decade of service with the St. Louis Pagan Picnic. She works on a regular basis hosting discussion and study groups and works throughout the year with her coven. She currently resides in Mid-Missouri with her husband and two children.*

Illustrator: Tim Foley

If You're Pagan, Why Don't I Like You?

Kerri Connor

As Pagans, we're told that we need to be more tolerant and enlightened than others. Some traditions encourage "harm none" or the rule of three (what you send out comes back times three), but you may come across someone, or several people, whom you simply cannot stand. Being around them, reading their comments, or hearing their voice might make your skin crawl.

Chances are this has happened to you. You may have hidden it, because you felt guilty. You may have tried to justify your feelings. You may even have felt confused and wondered if you were being tested by a higher power.

Perhaps it happened at a large festival or in a small, private group, or perhaps it happened online, on a Facebook page, or in an e-mail group. Maybe it hasn't happened to you yet, but chances are it will someday: you will find yourself wondering about someone, "If you're Pagan, why don't I like you?"

You really don't have to force yourself to like everybody, and there are probably plenty of people out there whom you shouldn't like. If someone makes you uncomfortable and you don't feel right around them, stay away from them. Your body is telling you what your mind is trying to deny.

I was once friends with a woman and her husband who owned a local shop. A few months after we met, the shop owners' coven stopped meeting and several of the members began practicing with my grove— the owners as well.

If someone makes you uncomfortable and you don't feel right around them, stay away from them. Your body is telling you what your mind is trying to deny.

When they suddenly decided to sell the shop, I looked into buying it, but it didn't feel right. Though I had always dreamed of owning a shop, I took a pass, and thank the Goddess I did. Turned out the store needed a good bailing out, which would have bankrupted my family.

By this time, I was starting to look more deeply at this friendship. Some things just didn't seem right to me, but I thought I was being too picky.

Our friendship continued until one night when I had a party at my house and things got way out of hand. Items were broken and stolen, and though it was my home and property, these people made me feel as though it was all my fault. After several months, I ended up being the one to apologize, even though I knew I really had been the victim. We began talking again, but things quickly went downhill.

Election time was coming, and suddenly this couple, who previously had shown no interest in politics, became very political. They joined the ranks of the Tea Party, and didn't see the irony. One of their own coven members, who had been openly gay for years, was now being publicly bashed by the wife. The wife would post terrible things on Facebook and then delete them so her husband wouldn't know, and then would claim she had never done it. We were shocked that they believed our (future) president was not an

American and that minorities and gays should have no rights. Their previous attitude of "coexist" became one of hatred against Muslims, and money became a major topic of conversation. All the time they still claimed they were Pagans who practiced "harm none."

Someone I had seen as a spiritual person turned into someone who drank and smoked all the time, appeared to like taking advantage of people, showed no respect for those with different beliefs, and became downright aggressive toward those with different political and sexual views and those with a different racial background. She couldn't have become more of my opposite. I knew that with her beliefs, we were too far apart on the spectrum ever to be friends again. I simply did not like her anymore. She could call herself Pagan all she wanted, but in all my years I had never met a Pagan who acted in this manner. I felt it was an insult to my faith and to all the Pagans I knew. Yet to her, she was still a Pagan.

After I told her I didn't want her in my life, things started going wrong: lost work, lost items, unexplainable illnesses, and a bizarre letter from a mutual friend telling me we couldn't be friends because of *my* radical political beliefs (apparently being a Democrat is highly radical these days, and this letter seemed even more odd due to the fact that it was written months after the election). Friends who had told me before they didn't like her were suddenly her fans, though they couldn't explain why. It was as if a giant mass of negativity was following me around and some of my friends were becoming brainwashed!

Since I seldom do readings for myself, I turned to five friends who didn't know this woman for help. All five psychics said that not only was she very angry at me, but they believed she had done some sort of hex or spell against me. An aura photo showed what looked like arrows attacking the right side of my body. The psychics all stated that I had definitely had encounters with this woman in a past life.

It's been a long process, but I believe she is now about 98 percent out of my life. I removed not only anything she ever gave to me, but also anything I bought in her store and still had. I did protection spell after protection spell and went through a lot of salt and moon water.

There are people who have told me, "Oh, you just need to forgive and forget, and give her love and light." Well, I did that, several times, and only ended up getting burned worse. Doing the same thing over and over again and expecting different results is not the definition of love, it's the definition of insanity.

Besides, why should I be forced to like someone who has completely different morals and ideals than I do? I don't judge people based on their race or sexual orientation, but, I admit, I will judge the people that do, and my verdict is that I don't want people like that in my life. Pagan or not, if you treat people badly, I don't want you around me.

While my experience with this person may seem like an extreme example, you may encounter someone who simply rubs you the wrong way and makes you feel uncomfortable. Listen to that signal!

There were many issues in my relationship with this woman that didn't work. There was what I saw as her hypocrisy—telling others how to live but not living that way herself. There was the sneakiness

of hiding what she said to others on Facebook by deleting comments quickly so she could deny ever posting them. There was the bigotry shown against minority races and gays. There was the public abuse and betrayal of her own family and supposed friends. There was the belief that this woman and I had had poor relationships in our past lives. Now, even if I wasn't Pagan and I found myself having these same issues with someone else, I still wouldn't like the person and I wouldn't feel like I should have to. Being Pagan doesn't mean I have to like every single person I meet. We teach coexistence, but coexistence doesn't mean you have to allow yourself to be a doormat.

Being Pagan doesn't mean I have to like every single person I meet. We teach coexistence, but coexistence doesn't mean you have to allow yourself to be a doormat.

"Coexist" simply means we need to exist within the same time and space as others in peace. That peace may come in the form of friendship, but it doesn't have to. It doesn't mean we have to love everyone else, but we do have to tolerate them to an extent. Sometimes living in peace with someone requires nothing more than ignoring them.

On the other side of the fence, for years I had thought of attending some of the larger local festivals. I joined Facebook groups where I could connect with others who were looking to attend and many who had already attended for years. I had come to understand that one particular event I was interested in had a camping area that was reserved for those who preferred nudity all the time. While it's not my thing, I figured since they were off in their own area and not walking around nude in front of children (knowing full well how the state authorities would see that!), it didn't really concern me.

But then I found out I was wrong. I had been given the wrong information: nudity was allowed anywhere on the grounds except by the gates, where someone outside of the campground might see and report it. I voiced my concerns about the law, about the fact that no one wanted outsiders to know, and about children seeing people they don't know wandering around naked, and was immediately told that I couldn't be a real Pagan if I wasn't willing to back them up. Almost thirty years of practicing, and people who didn't know me told me I couldn't be a real Pagan because I didn't want to expose my naked body to children or be a part of allowing others to. I was also told that this festival, which was supposed to be "welcoming to all," wasn't for me. They got that part right.

However, not wanting to expose my naked body to someone else's children does not make me less of a Pagan. It does make me a law-abiding adult. I suppose some people have an issue with that, but that is their problem, not mine. Being Pagan does not make me above the laws of my state. It also doesn't mean that I think young kids should be exposed to the nudity of strangers. And it certainly does not make me any less Pagan to believe these things.

These people had made up their minds about me knowing only one piece of information about me—the fact that I didn't think children should be exposed to the nudity of strangers. So whether they realize it or not, they also judge people on their beliefs, and I'm okay with that. I would have been far more upset if I had spent the hundreds of dollars to go to this event only to find out once I got there that it definitely was not the place for me.

It is getting to the point that we are being told we can't be Pagan and disagree with one another, and that is ridiculous. When someone runs around saying that all the things you believe in are bad, there really is no law requiring you to like that person, whether they are Pagan or not. You don't have to feel guilt. You just need to understand what you want in your life and what you don't and realize you have the right to decide. Being Pagan doesn't mean you must like all other Pagans, just as being a certain race doesn't mean you have to like all other members of that race. "Pagan" is only part of who we are, and it varies from person to person. Pagan means many things to many people these days, and to very few does it mean its original definition of being a country dweller (which I am). Dictionaries don't even agree on the definition of Pagan anymore.

Because "Pagan" means so many different things, we have to look at the actions of the person instead, not their "title" of Pagan. If those actions give you a bad vibe, that's all you really

Being Pagan doesn't mean you must like all other Pagans, just as being a certain race doesn't mean you have to like all other members of that race. "Pagan" is only part of who we are, and it varies from person to person.

need to know. Follow what your heart is telling you, and you will find yourself surrounded by people you not only like but genuinely love.

Kerri Connor *is the author of* The Pocket Spell Creator, The Pocket Guide to Rituals, The Pocket Idiot's Guide to Potions, Goodbye Grandmother, *and* Spells for Tough Times *and is the former editor of* The Circle of Stones Journal. *Kerri is the High Priestess of The Gathering Grove and has been practicing her craft for twenty-six years. She dances under the moon in rural Illinois.*

Illustrator: Christa Marquez

The Audacity of Subscribing to the Unfashionable Idea of "Harm None"

Mickie Mueller

First off, I'm no fluffy bunny who believes the universe is all white light and rainbows. But I do strive to harm none in my magical practice as well as in my mundane life, much to the chagrin of many of the magical practitioners I know.

Some people are of the belief that the practice of "harm none" magically ties your hands and keeps you from being able to work magic for your own success or to shield yourself from baneful magic and negativity. I've seen eye-rolling and the all too familiar scoff at the very mention of the Rede, which includes ideals that only ten to fifteen years ago

I've noticed a trend in the Pagan community over the last several years where some people are starting to think that if you're a serious, hardcore Witch, no rules are necessary.

were considered commonplace among magical practitioners. I've noticed a trend in the Pagan community over the last several years where some people are starting to think that if you're a serious, hardcore Witch, no rules are necessary.

I've discovered through my personal magical path, however, that following the tenet of harm none simply means that you become more mindful of *how* to achieve your goals, but you do not become limited in how to achieve them. I have discovered both challenges and rewards in navigating the complexities of the deceptively simple concept of harm none while living a magical life.

What Does "Harm None" Mean to You?

First of all, "harm none" is a concept that many people want to simplify, but it was never meant to be simple. It was meant to make you think, consider your actions, and work toward the best solutions for all involved. In order to have some understanding of this, we need only look to the founders of modern Wicca, who were the first to tout the concept of harm none. Many of these Witches of England were also credited with working magic against the Nazi invasion shortly before the Battle of Britain. That doesn't sound like the work of a bunch of shrinking violets who can't hold their own, so why do many Witches today look at the concept as being wishy-washy or limiting? The answer probably lies in a misunderstanding of the complexities of "harm none."

Harm can come from both action and inaction. Those of us who try our best to live the concept of harm none weigh our choices all the time. Does that mean we always manage to do the right thing? Nope. But when discussing spirituality, we must remember that the journey is often more valuable than the destination,

and it's the mindfulness, the attempt to follow a path, that's important. If we stumble or trip, then we learn, and we will do better next time.

Dealing with Challenging Situations

So, if you harm none, does that mean you can't kill bugs in your house? Protect yourself from a stalker? Pull weeds from your garden? Again, it's important to remember that you can cause harm through inaction as well as action. If I have one spider in the bathtub, I catch it under a glass and release it into the garden. But an invasion of many spiders means my family's safety is in danger, so it would cause more harm in the long run not to exterminate the intruders. I can't allow my family to come to harm, first and foremost. We have to pull weeds to protect the plants we're trying to cultivate. If you were in a dark alley and were attacked, would you just allow it to happen? That kind of inaction is not why the concept of harm none exists. We should never allow ourselves or our loved ones to come to harm if we can prevent it, and believe me, if I had to, I would fight back, because I would be preventing harm from coming to myself.

How Harming None Helps Your Magic Grow

In order to better explain how we can meet the challenge of acting through magic while still maintaining the commitment to harming none, I'll share a couple of examples.

I once received a frantic phone call from a Witch friend of mine who was about to graduate and had learned about a job opportunity at a gallery that was only available for a short time. He explained that he needed to get some paperwork from his college right away in order even to be considered for the position. He was in his car on the way to the office at the time, with no way to whip up some magic on his own.

He said, "I know you do all that 'harm none' stuff, but I really need your help! The only one in the office is Sally Jones, and she never gives me what I want! Can you put the magic mojo on her for me so she'll give me the paperwork? I really need this job!"

"Don't worry, I've got this," I told him in a reassuring tone.

I had no intention of putting the magic mojo on Sally Jones. I knew I could manage it without coercing anyone to act against their will. I had permission from my friend to do magic for him, so I worked a quick spell while visualizing him walking out of the office with a big beaming grin on his face, his paperwork in hand. I got a call half an hour later.

"Hey, it turns out I didn't need that spell after all! Remember the dean of the college who bought a painting from my student art show? He was in the office and Sally Jones was out to lunch! He got me my paperwork personally and gave me a letter of recommendation, too! I never see him in the office. I guess I was just lucky!"

By making the decision not to zap ol' Sally and visualizing the outcome that my friend wanted, I was able to help him get more than he had hoped for. Since magic takes the path of least resistance, the best person to help him was there, and he got an outcome that might not have been available with a short-sighted spell that disregarded another person's free will. It's not that hard if you just think it through.

Here's another example. While living in a small neighborhood, I left my car unlocked and my GPS was stolen right in my driveway. I called the police, who told me there had been a rash of break-ins in the area. I was sure I would never see my GPS again. My knee-jerk reaction was to send out the flying monkeys to find whoever did it and give them a nasty pentagram-shaped rash. Instead, I took a day to calm down. I did my magic with a cool head, and the entire purpose of the spell was to recover my GPS. One week later I got a call from the police. They had busted the thief and found my GPS undamaged, along with the property of several other people as well. Had I not resisted the urge to lash out at the perpetrator, something bad might have happened to the thief that might have prevented the recovery of my wayward tech device. In this instance, the universe followed the path of least resistance once again, and the simplest way to get my GPS back was for the bad guy to get busted.

. . . .

Never underestimate Witches who follow "harm none." They find power in their practices and can be magical powerhouses as they walk the path of their spiritual calling.

Mickie Mueller *is an award-winning and critically acclaimed artist of fantasy, fairy, and myth. She enjoys creating magical art full of fairies, goddesses, and beings of folklore. She works primarily in a mix of colored pencil and watercolor infused with magical herbs corresponding to her subject matter. Mickie is the illustrator of* The Well Worn Path *and* The Hidden Path *decks, the writer/illustrator of* Voice of the Trees: A Celtic Divination Oracle, *and the illustrator of the* Mystical Cats Tarot. *Mickie is a regular contributor to several of the Llewellyn annuals. Visit her online at www.mickiemuellerart.com.*

Illustrator: Jennifer Hewitson

Witchy Living

DAY-BY-DAY WITCHCRAFT

The Practice of Gratitude

Dallas Jennifer Cobb

If the only prayer you ever said was thank you, that would be enough.
—Meister Eckhart

L iving a magical life, I have a lot of rituals, routines, and rites that help to shape my life, but of all the things I do to create and sustain a magical life, the practice of gratitude has probably been the one thing that has had the most profound and lasting effect.

The practice of gratitude is a finite and powerful form of magic that produces great results. Whether you use it to attract abundance and wealth, to call

If magic is the ability to change energy at will, then the practice of gratitude is pure magic, altering energy easily and fluidly and producing amazing results.

in your soul mate, to create a safe and happy environment, or to achieve your deepest desires, the practice of gratitude is something that can radically alter your life. And, if magic is the ability to change energy at will, then the practice of gratitude is pure magic, altering energy easily and fluidly and producing amazing results.

Last summer, during a particularly trying time in my life, I was searching for something to help me feel even a little better. A friend suggested writing a gratitude list, reminding me of the age-old proverb "Whatever we focus on grows." And that was the beginning of my practice of gratitude. The simple list helped me to shift my bad feelings in the moment, turning my awareness to the good things in my life.

Inspired by the instant effectiveness of this technique, I began to make a daily gratitude list, and also sought out information and resources on the subject. I learned a variety of techniques and practices that helped me to focus on and give thanks for the goodness in so many areas of my life. I found ways to cultivate gratitude for the wonders of nature, the blessings of the universe, the kindness of people, and the miracles of everyday life. These practices changed my perspective and focus, lifting me out of the worry, stress, and anger that surrounded the difficult situation I was working through and enabling me to feel happy, joyous, and well supported.

I learned quickly about the Law of Attraction, one of the universal laws derived from physics, which states, "Like attracts like." If I was wallowing in fear, anger, victimhood, or self-pity, that was more likely what I would attract, but if I shifted my attention to gratitude for things both tangible and intangible, then I would in turn attract more of them. And that sounded good to me.

I expanded my practice of gratitude, trying many different forms. Some worked better than others, and these I made into regular practices. I want to share some of these and spread the magic and goodness around. Because everyone could use a little more magic in life.

The Research Says...

The practice of gratitude has been shown to shift body-based energy, eliciting an effect similar to the "relaxation response." A wide variety of studies have been done on the topic, so if you are a "show me and I will believe" sort of person, here is some of the proof. If magic is the practice of changing energy at will, then the measurement of that change is proof of the magic at work.

Research has shown that meditation and prayer produce a relaxation response within the human body. Pulse and respiration rates lower, as do oxygen consumption rates and blood lactate levels.[1] More recent research has shown that neural structures in the brain and nervous system are activated by meditation, prayer, and affirmation, specifically those structures that are involved in attention and control of the autonomic nervous system. More recent research into the effects of vibrational medicine documents the energy change that occurs within the body with the practice of gratitude and affirmation.[2]

Like meditation and prayer, the practice of gratitude has been shown to induce the relaxation response, reduce systolic blood pressure, and improve sleep quality. Studies have also shown that a person's level of gratitude positively correlates to their level of vitality and energy, and the frequency of their gratitude practice positively correlates to their increased perception of well-being.[3]

What Experience Says

When I first started making simple gratitude lists, I was a bit of a doubter, but by the end of the first list, I was a believer. Turning my attention to what was working in my life, and away from the contemplation of my problems, actually made me feel better. My stomach relaxed, my headache lessened, and I felt a little shiver of excitement. Yes, I thought, *there really is a lot of goodness surrounding me.*

That increased awareness of the goodness that existed in my life energized me and gave me hope. I felt better physically and started to think about solutions rather than just problems. To anyone who has felt stressed, sick to their stomach, or plagued by a headache (either literally or figuratively), the cessation of the sick sensation comes as a delight.

Relieved by the reduction of the symptoms of stress, I decided that practicing gratitude was a solution to how overwhelmed I had been feeling. Everything in my body, my gut instinct, said that focusing on gratitude made me feel better physically, mentally, and emotionally. I was convinced.

Gratitude Basics

So what is gratitude, and how do you practice it? A quick quip will tell you that "gratitude is an attitude." But let's take a moment and consider what gratitude really is.

Growing up, we were all taught manners. We were taught to say please and thank you, expressing our desire and gratitude for what was provided to us. We didn't take things for granted. As adults, these simple good manners are still useful in every situation, but the cultivated practice of gratitude moves us beyond common courtesy and into the realm of cultivating a state of mind and a way of life that is truly thankful for what we receive.

Gratitude is the practice of consciously turning your attention to what is good in yourself, in your life, in your community, and in the world. It is the practice of saying thank you not just to people, but to the universe. A practice of gratitude is the process of paying attention in the moment, noticing what is given to us, and uttering that one little prayer: *Thank you.*

A practice of gratitude is the process of paying attention in the moment, noticing what is given to us, and uttering that one little prayer: *Thank you.*

The Law of Attraction

Early on in my practice, I read a lot about the Law of Attraction. Sadly, much of what's written these days is about financial abundance, and while I never turn down more money, the source of my problem was not money-based, so much of the literature didn't quite hit the mark.

A friend facing a terminal illness shifted everything for me. He said he was grateful for his illness, which made him very aware of all the goodness he enjoyed every day. "Sunlight on my face feels like an exquisite gift," he told me. That woke me up. Like the teenage saying "YOLO" (you only live once), I began to see each day as a gift—one for which I could choose how I would experience it. I could remain mired in problems and complaints, or, like my friend who was facing death, I could be grateful for each small blessing.

I started paying more attention and thanking people who gave me something lovely. I remember my daughter's surprised face when I thanked her for hugging me in the morning. And I can still see the shocked face of the cook who stood behind the food service area in the big hotel dining room. I caught her eye and said, "Thank you. It is so nice to have breakfast made for me." She laughed, leaned toward me, and said, "No one's ever thanked me before. And I've worked here for nine years. You made my day." We both walked away from the exchange smiling.

There are so many places to express our gratitude, especially for things that often go unthanked: people in invisible positions (like the cook) who serve me daily, the garbage collector, the traffic cop, the person at the drive-through window, and the cashier in the grocery store. I thank them when I see them, or give thanks for them when I don't see them. My gratitude keeps me aware of all they do that contributes to my life.

Daily Tools

I use several daily tools to cultivate gratitude. Each has its own effect. I use a morning moment to focus myself for the day, in-the-moment awareness to cultivate gratitude minute by minute, and pre-blessing practice to shape upcoming situations. And I count my blessings at the end of the day.

When I wake up in the morning, I stretch and give thanks: *I'm grateful to be awake and refreshed, and happy to be alive and healthy. I'm filled with gratitude for a new day in which everything is possible.* This moment helps to set my internal tone for the day. I'm focused on the good, and open to the infinite possibilities the day holds.

Minute-by-minute gratitude requires awareness. It's easy to remember when good things happen, but the more I use this technique, the more I find gratitude in most minutes of the day. Whatever the situation I find myself in, it is easy to find something about it to give thanks for. *I'm grateful for this food I'm eating, and thankful to live in an area rich in agriculture and blessed by an abundance of fresh, local, and healthy food. Thank you for foods that are good for me and taste good.*

When I have stressful, worrisome, or difficult situations scheduled for the day ahead, I take time to pre-bless the situation before I enter into it. Say, for example, that I have a dental appointment in the afternoon. I am anxious about the dentist, so rather than succumb entirely to the anxiety, aggravating my nervous system and causing more internalized stress, I use a gratitude practice to pre-bless the situation. In as much detail as possible, I envision myself leaving home, traveling joyfully and safely in the car, and arriving at the dentist's office a little early and at ease. I see myself in the dentist's chair and envision his smiling face looking down at me. The dentist is saying, "Your teeth look great! Let's just do a little polish and you'll be all done." In the greatest amount of detail possible, I walk myself through the situation in my mind, and invoke good outcomes to the situation, pre-blessing it before it happens.

Before sleeping at night, I count my blessings. I make note of every lovely, unexpected thing that happened to me during the day, such as money found, checks received in the mail, sweet greetings and compliments from people, joy and laughter experienced throughout the day, and even the occurrence of beauty and nature. By writing down what I am grateful for, thankful for, and blessed by, I make lists of all the goodness I experienced throughout the day. I see tangibly how rich I am.

Gratitude in Tough Times

Sure, it's easy to be grateful when the going is good, but what about practicing gratitude in hard times, with difficult people, or during a crisis?

A family member of mine died suddenly last year, which resulted in waves of chaos and grief washing throughout the extended family. I found it very stressful—not just the event and the fallout, but having to replay the emotions over and over as people processed their reactions.

We know through the Law of Attraction that bad feelings beget more bad feelings, so in order to survive the family gatherings, the

funeral home visitation, and the funeral, I needed to find a way to shift the energy that surrounded the situation. And gratitude helped me to do this.

Oh sure, you say, what is there to be grateful for about death? And that was what I asked of the situation: *What is there to be grateful for?* I found many things.

Before he died, my brother-in-law spent an evening telling funny stories with his brother. They hung out in the "man cave," watched a hockey game, ate stinky cheese, farted, and told funny stories. His brother stayed the night, and they shared coffee and breakfast in the morning. Two hours later, my brother-in-law had chest pain, called 911, coded out in the ambulance, and, after almost two hours spent trying to revive him, was pronounced dead.

Where is the gratitude in this?

I am grateful that my brother-in-law's last day was filled with sibling love, that he was not alone despite his spouse being away overnight. I am thankful that he laughed and told stories and enjoyed good food and company. And most of all, I am glad that he went quickly and wasn't left to linger in a severely disabled state. He died quickly, after a loving visit. And for this, I am truly grateful.

Even in the most difficult situations, we can always find something to be thankful for, if we look for it. Gratitude is an attitude, but one we have to learn to cultivate.

Living in Gratitude

Gratitude has a miraculous effect on our lives, manifesting and attracting more goodness, and alchemically altering us in the realms of physical, emotional, mental, and social reality. By employing the Law of Attraction, practicing gratitude can actually help to draw more goodness to us, as like attracts like, and good will attracts good.

By cultivating awareness, we begin noticing what we receive, and through the expression of thanks, we welcome more of that person, place, thing, or experience to our lives.

Resources on Gratitude

You can read about the latest research on the effects of gratitude in the books *Thanks! How the New Science of Gratitude Can Make You Happier*, by Robert Emmons (Jossey-Bass, 2013), and *Living Life as a Thank You: The Transformative Power of Daily Gratitude*, by Nina Lesowitz (Viva Editions, 2009).

For help and inspiration to develop your own gratitude practice, I recommend *The Magic*, by Rhonda Byrne (Atria Books, 2012).

Or maybe you want a phone app to make a gratitude list on the go. Happytapper.com has a variety of apps designed for just this purpose, including an app for gratitude journaling, an app for creating a vision board, and even an app full of inspirational quotes to uplift you when you need it.

There are tons of gratitude resources available, but the easiest and cheapest of them all is that simple prayer: *Thank you.*

Notes

1. R. Jevning, R. K. Wallace, and M. Beidebach, "The Physiology of Meditation: A Review," *Neuroscience & Biobehavioral Reviews* 16 (1992): 415.

2. Dr. Richard Gerber, *Vibrational Medicine* (Rochester, VT: Bear & Co., 2001), pp. 39–44.

3. R. Emmons and M. McCulloch, "Counting Blessings Versus Burdens," *Journal of Personality and Social Psychology* vol. 84, no. 2 (2003): 377-99.

Dallas Jennifer Cobb *practices gratitude magic, giving thanks for her magical life, happy and healthy family, meaningful and flexible work, and joyous life. She believes the Goddess will provide time, energy, wisdom, and money to accomplish all her deepest desires. She lives in paradise, in a waterfront village in rural Ontario, and chants: "Thank you, thank you, thank you." Contact her at jennifer.cobb@live.com.*

Illustrator: Bri Hermanson

Urban Magic

Reverend J. Variable x/ø

What comes to mind when you envision Pagan lifestyles and magical workings? A circle of Druids dancing around a bonfire in the deep woods beneath a starlit sky? A rustic crone tending her garden? A wizened beast-master communing with the animals in a sunlit meadow?

How about a graffiti artist spray-painting magical tags on the walls of a trash-filled alley, bards performing on electronic instruments at a crowded downtown festival, or a few coven mates basking in the pulsing, buzzing power of an electrical transformer?

The word *Pagan* originally meant "country dweller." Over the centuries, the term has also come to encompass the spiritual beliefs and practices of our pastoral ancestors. In the old days, large cities were few and far between, and travel was time-consuming and dangerous. Most people spent their entire lives on farms or in small villages on the edge of a vast wilderness. The magic and lore that we think of as "Pagan" developed as people learned how to survive and thrive in the wild, capricious, and often dangerous bosom of Mother Nature.

Fast-forward to today. The number of humans in the world has increased at an alarmingly exponential rate. As of 2010, according to the World Health Organization, roughly half of these humans are living in major urban centers rather than in the tight-knit rural communities of the past. It's a testimony to the proud Pagan legacy that so many of the old practices and beliefs persist to this day, in the face of religious persecution, the Scientific Enlightenment, and the Industrial Revolution.

Just as our ancestors were immersed from birth in a world of endless forests and fields, most of today's Pagans are children of the city, and feel perfectly in tune with the metropolitan energy and spirit.

Life as a country dweller is no longer feasible for every Witch and Wizard, though. New eras bring new possibilities and perspectives. Just as our ancestors were immersed in a world of endless forests and fields, most of today's Pagans are children of the city, and feel perfectly in tune with the metropolitan energy and spirit.

Urban Magic: Metromancy

The setting may be different, but the essence of Pagan spirituality and magical tradition endures. The modern mage still honors the old ways by adapting these ancient techniques and ideas to new environments and situations.

SOURCES OF ENERGY

Cities contain a wide variety of energy nodes and currents of all different frequencies and flavors. With a little practice, it's easy to locate and identify the many individual vibrations that are available and tap into this power for your own spellwork. While you probably don't want to perform major rituals in public (or maybe you do! Cities often have festivals and other events at which such displays are appropriate), you can store this energy for future use, or tap into it to subtly weave magical threads throughout all of your daily activities. With a little common sense and decorum, you'll develop your own unobtrusive magical style and be able to apply your skills anywhere, anytime.

Think about all the different types of energy that you use, or could use, in your magical work. Do you commonly generate this energy from within yourself, perhaps with the help of a few tokens from a table of correspondences? Consider letting your city supply you with some of that raw power. Everywhere you go, you'll find vibrating nodes, hubs, and currents available for the taking. There's no moral quandary here—you needn't siphon anyone else's personal life force or detract from another's experience of a moment. The energy of a public place is freely generated by all participants and is available to everyone. Making use of it is like lighting your personal torch at a community bonfire.

Energy of Archetypes and Deities
Wherever people repeatedly gather for a specific purpose, their focus constantly reinforces vibrations that attract the deities who rule over that purpose, whether that ground is officially consecrated to them or not. The urban mage knows how to take advantage of the various sacred spaces available throughout the city.

Need to connect with a god of war? Chant your mantra as you attend a heated sporting event or dive into a mosh pit at your local metal/punk club. If you desire the romantic passion of Eros, Aphrodite, or their colleagues, a dance club might be the place to tune in. If you seek a love that runs deeper and lasts longer, soak up the ambiance of a wedding party as they make their joyous exit from the church or other sacred space at the conclusion of their ceremony. The campus of your local university is a great place to commune with the spirits of wisdom and academia, and if you need money, contact the pecuniary deities by conducting a quick, quiet ritual while waiting in line at the bank.

Temporal Energy

Every town is full of stories, and stories hold some powerful magic. Go through the old documents, newspapers, photographs, and maps in your library and town records. Get a feel for how things used to be and how they have changed throughout the years. What are some of the historic markers, and what happened there? Where did the old train tracks go? Was that cul de sac always a dead end, or is there an old road hidden beneath the new construction? When the potholes peel the asphalt away, what can you learn from the old cobblestones lurking beneath? Who is buried in the cemeteries, and what secrets might they have to share?

The echoes of the past continue to reverberate in the present. Take advantage of them.

Energy Currents

The technological age has immersed us in a thick soup of electromagnetic fields and energy waves. Wireless signals, electric lines, and power plants are obvious sources of raw energy that's there for the taking. Movement, too, induces powerful energy currents, and the channels along which these currents travel have long been a part of magical lore. Legends and spells are full of rivers, roads, and pathways. There's plenty of kinetic energy to work with in the city!

Go and stand on the side of a freeway overpass or underpass while the cars zip by above or below, and see if you can get a feel for the energy generated by the traffic, the hum of the tires, and the thoughts of the passengers as they move toward their destinations. Find the point between the lanes and see if you can sense the balance in forces as the energy flows in both directions on either side of you. If you're lucky enough to live near a point where several freeways meet, see if you can sense the magical buzzing in the air around the knot of ramps and overpasses.

This energy can be used as a carrier wave, much like a river, or absorbed and stored in an amulet for future use. When you send out your own energy of intent, take advantage of what's already there, and let it add force and momentum to your own intentions.

Natural Energy

No matter how much we urban mages like our asphalt and shiny lights, it's still good to get around the green stuff now and then. One of the best features of city life is simple: urban mages have a choice of environments. Just because you're in the city doesn't mean you can't hug a tree. Even if you don't have a yard of your own, you can take advantage of the city parks and public gardens. Notice all the natural life thriving even in the heart of your downtown area. Trees beautify the sidewalks. Birds flock everywhere. If you have an affinity for plant life, see if you can connect with the urban growth. Do city plants have a different "feel" than their country cousins? What can they tell you about the magic that runs deep in the urban earth beneath the streets and sidewalks where they've put down their roots?

SACRED GEOMETRY

Math is the first language of the universe. Sacred geometry is a physical manifestation of the abstract power of number. Certainly there are countless examples of this found in nature—the number of petals on a blossom, the spiral of branches around a tree trunk, the fractal self-similarity of rivers, trees, and rock formations—but the city's human-made structures and design carry the esoteric power of number and geometry as well.

Examine the construction of the buildings, the carefully planned landscaping, and the layout of the roads. See what kinds of shapes you can draw in the maps when you connect important sites or your own favorite landmarks. Can you spot larger patterns and shapes in the grid? What about the numerology of the angles, intersections, and distance ratios?

Now imagine performing your spellwork at these specific places around town, drawing on the energy of the location, its history and mathematical precision, surrounded by all the currents generated by the kinetic motion of the traffic as it flows around you. Send the energy out right away to do your will, or absorb it into a talisman to be used later. The city is a power plant—plug in and charge up!

Treasure Hunt

Where there's life, there's litter, whether it's the cast-off flora and fauna of the woodlands or the human-generated detritus rattling around in the streets and alleyways of an urban jungle. Of course we humans (should) try to keep things clean, but there's no denying that the dystopian clutter adds a nice gritty ambiance to the cityscape. Some people truly thrive in settings like this.

What's more, that unsightly mess is a treasure trove of magical potential. Pay attention, and you'll uncover material for "found art" projects, magical tools and amulets in the rough, odd trinkets for your mojo bag, and now and then a perfectly serviceable object that you can clean up and keep for yourself or sell for some quick cash.

DIVINATION

If you're sensitive to signs and portents, you'll find that the urban landscape is full of information on many different layers. Pose a question and get out there. As you move through the streets, keep your dreaming eyes open and pay attention to the subtext in the language of your city as it mutters to itself: the odd sign or graffiti symbol, overheard snippets of conversation, the headline in last month's newspaper that flies across your path—all that chaos is full of messages.

Metropolitan Druids

A bustling city provides a spectrum of options for social interaction and activities. For many rural Pagans, isolation is a double-edged sword. While it's fine for the solitary practitioner who likes it that way, life in the country can often make it hard to meet new people, schedule gatherings, and perform group work. City mages can make use of bulletin boards, Pagan community centers, mass transit, and nearby libraries and specialty shops. Covens and informal magical groups often have a presence on the Internet, too, and some will issue open invitations to similar-minded folks seeking camaraderie and connections.

THE SPIRIT OF THE CITY

The "concrete jungle" is an apt metaphor. The city is full of life, organic and otherwise. Take a walk through a busy urban area and open your magical senses to the energies to be found along the way. Every building has its own personality. Different neighborhoods emit different frequencies. A small bookstore has one vibration, a chain coffee shop franchise another. Traffic ebbs and flows to the beat of the stoplights. Rush hour comes and goes. Night and day bring their own particular atmospheres and magical possibilities.

Pay attention to the aura surrounding different blocks, individual buildings, public artwork, construction zones, shops, tourist attractions… Everything in the city is buzzing with life and spirit, whether it's technically alive or not.

One basic foundation of Pagan belief that has not changed over time is the idea that everything is alive and sentient, from each individual tree, herb, river, and rock to the elements themselves. Ancient lore and magical wisdom developed as we began to understand and communicate with the spirits of the natural world around us. If everything has a spirit of its own, why should cities be any different?

Reverend J. Variable x/ø *is good with shapes, words, sounds, light, shadows, numbers, and ideas. Her family consists of one excellent husband, a fine yellow snake, several computers, two sarcastic automobiles, the houseplants that she keeps finding by the dumpster whenever someone moves out of her apartment complex, and any spiders who happen to wander into the house. Her influences include Frank Zappa, Neil Gaiman, and Connie Dobbs. She lives on the Internet at www.grimagix.com, www.dreamsoverzero.com, and www.reverendvariable.com. In meatspace, she can often be found reading Tarot cards in the quieter taverns and cafes of Portland, Oregon. She frequently has to remind herself to use the Oxford comma.*

Illustrator: Tim Foley

Building Magickal Community

Emily Carlin

Over the last decade or so, the number of people identifying as magickal practitioners has increased exponentially. Seeing such growth, one might assume that our local magickal communities have grown and strengthened at the same rate, and yet that is not the case. Somewhere between 60 and 80 percent of Pagans identify as solitaries these days rather than being a part of a local group (Pitzl-Waters). This is due in large part to the easy availability of information on magickal practice in books and online. One no longer needs to find an in-person teacher or be accepted into a community before learning to practice magick. All that's required is a library card or access to the Internet. However, just because someone comes into the Craft on their own doesn't mean that they don't want to be part of a larger community. A glance at any forum for magickal people will just about always reveal at least a half-dozen calls for meetups, rituals, or study groups. If you're looking for community, you're not alone.

A glance at any forum for magickal people will just about always reveal at least a half-dozen calls for meetups, rituals, or study groups. If you're looking for community, you're not alone.

Sadly, this amazing growth has actually made creating magickal community more difficult rather than less. When people have to go to established communities and teachers to find their way into magickal practice, they learn certain common practices, etiquette, and protocols—things like waiting to be cut out of a circle, being careful to pronounce a chant the way others do, or learning certain songs. This essentially builds commonalities between practitioners, making it easier for them to find common ground on which to build connection and community. Today, with so many practitioners custom-building their Craft, taking elements from an incredible variety of sources and putting their own spin on them, there is far less commonality that can be taken for granted. Not all practitioners wear the same clothes and know the same chants or rituals, and they certainly don't hold the same beliefs. This means it can take a lot more effort to build real community.

Benefits of Community

So what is "real community"? For most magickal practitioners, real community means a place where we can openly practice our Craft and where we can be accepted for who and what we really are; where we don't have to hide or pretend to be something we're not. Such acceptance requires a great deal of openness and understanding from the larger group. This can be very difficult to achieve when practitioners of widely different practices and backgrounds try to come together. You've heard the joke about the ceremonialist and the Wiccan walking into a bar, right? It isn't made any easier by the fact that magickal practitioners in general tend to be fiercely individualistic and resistant to authority. There is a reason that organizing magickal folks is often referred to as herding cats. And yet, despite all our differences, we still want to come together.

In all our wondrous variety, magickal people have a lot to offer one another in a community. We may come from diverse backgrounds, practice different things, and hold different (or even conflicting) beliefs, but we share a certain spark. We share the knowledge that magick is real. That is no small thing to have in common. We can offer each other support and understanding that most mundane folk cannot really understand or provide. Whether it's getting a Tarot reading when you really need one, getting help with a house blessing, or receiving a cleansing, there are certain things that just require help from another magickal person. A long-distance or online friend can help you come up with an invocation or even impart energy from a distance (if they're very good), but no matter their skill, they cannot help you craft a cord or bless a new baby. This is where being part of a local community is irreplaceable.

Joining a Community

Attempting to join a local community for the first time can be an intimidating experience. Groups have varying degrees of openness and acceptance of strangers. If you're fortunate enough to have a very open local community, just showing up to a few events may be enough to have the others embracing you as one of their own. If not, you will probably have to attend several open events and get to know the leaders before you're welcomed as a working member of the community. If that is the case, just be patient. If the community is worth joining, then it's worth the hoops you may have to jump through, and if it's not, then you will come away wiser and can try again with another group. Once you've found a group worth joining, there are many things you can do to help build and strengthen that community, even if you're a newcomer.

The single most important thing you can do for any gathering you ever join is to model the kind of behavior you want to see from the people around you. Do as you would be done by... sounds simple, doesn't it? And yet, how often do you find yourself at an event where you judge the people around you by how they dress, what symbols they wear, what books they've read, and who they know? How often do you actually behave in the open and respectful way in which you want others to behave? In actuality, fighting our prejudices and knee-jerk reactions is not that easy. Unless you've made a concerted effort to cultivate a sense of kindness, you will likely have to practice being open to the thoughts and opinions of others and respecting their beliefs, regardless of how much they may clash with your own.

If you do nothing else for your community, learn to cultivate a sense of respect for others. When it comes down to it, community isn't about everyone agreeing all the time (that's what cults are for), it's about being able to disagree respectfully and come to an accord anyway. Where there are multiple people, there will always be multiple opinions for the way things should be done or the way people should behave. You don't have to agree with everyone, but you do need to respect them. Take the time to listen to what they have to say and acknowledge their contributions, and show respect for the thoughts and feelings of those around you. Then, if you do disagree, it can be from a place of understanding and reason rather than prejudice. Community is a gift, and making the effort to truly understand and respect your fellow members honors that gift and makes the whole community a stronger, better place.

That same respect demands not only that you listen to others but that you communicate your thoughts and feelings clearly. One of the most common things that we all do to undermine and erode our communities is to not bring up potential problems out of a desire to avoid conflict. You may think you're being strong and bearing annoyance or pain for the good of the community, but you're not. A real community has conflicts but has the ability to deal with them as they arise. For any group to grow and thrive, it must be open to the needs of its members, but how is that possible when the community doesn't know what the needs of those people are? If you have a problem, it is your duty to bring it into the open to be addressed rather than to rot in the shadows. It may seem strange, but real community is strengthened by honest and respectful conflict—that's how it grows. Be brave and bring your troubles into the open to be healed.

Creating a New Community

But what if you can't find local community? Not all areas have strong magickal communities already, so sometimes you have to be bold and create them. If there are no groups holding events in your area, it may be time to step up and organize some. As intimidating as it may sound, if you're searching for community, chances are good that someone not too far from you is looking for it, too. Reserve the meeting room at your local library or Masonic lodge and have a ritual, try for a meetup at a local cafe or pub, organize a Craft or divination night, or organize a shopping trip to support local merchants. All it takes is determination and the willingness to go it alone if nobody else shows up. Recruit a friend to do it with you, and you've already got two. The worst that can happen is that no one shows up; that's not the end of the world. Be courageous and keep going until people start showing up. All communities start with an idea but are formed by elbow grease and determination.

Be brave. If you want to be part of a magickal community, you must be willing to be open and honest with the people around you, to show them the respect and consideration you want to receive, and to be brave enough to risk conflict to do the right thing. A real community isn't a place of perfect agreements and idyllic harmony. Instead, it's a place where your peers will confront you when you screw up and love and support you and fight to help you be better, and expect you to do the same for them. In its best form, magickal community is the family you choose.

Resources

Foundation for Community Encouragement. "Stages of Community Building." http://fce-community.org/stages-of-cb.

Hampton, Jerry L. Group Dynamics and Community Building. http://www.community4me.com/communitybldg1.html.

Peck, M. Scott. *The Different Drum: Community Making and Peace*. New York: Touchstone, 1987.

Pitzl-Waters, Jason. "Circling Alone: Paganism's Solitary Eclectic Future?" Patheos. http://www.patheos.com/blogs/wildhunt/2011/11/circling-alone-paganisms-solitary-eclectic-future.html.

Starhawk. *The Empowerment Manual: A Guide for Collaborative Groups*. Gabriola Island, BC: New Society Publishers, 2011.

Emily Carlin *is an eclectic witch and lawyer based in Seattle, Washington. She specializes in defensive magick, community building, and pop culture magick. Emily blogs at blacksunmagick.blogspot.com and teaches at Pagan events in the Puget Sound area. Defense Against the Dark, her first book, was published by New Page Books in March 2011. She can be reached via email at emily@e-carlin.com.*

Illustrator: Jennifer Hewitson

Sacred Self-Care: Interacting with Your Body in a Magical Way

Tess Whitehurst

It's an elementary concept that the way we feel—inside and out—has a powerful effect on every aspect of our lives. What's more, injecting a magical mindset into so-called mundane things can often reap the most lasting and profound magical rewards. Like water dripping on a stone, performing a practical ritual with magical reverence, day in and day out, can powerfully create new shapes and contours to the flow of our life momentum. As such, self-care practices—such as cleansing your body, brushing your teeth, and getting dressed—can be perfect vehicles for this kind of magic. Here, you'll discover a number of exquisitely simple, highly effective ways to infuse your everyday self-care practices with sacred attention and magical power.

Cleansing

Author Clarissa Pinkola Estes suggests thinking of the body as the "body consort," a loving friend and servant who provides for all your physical needs. Indeed, our bodies breathe for us and heal us even while we sleep. They let us know when we're hungry, tired, happy, satisfied, safe, or in danger. They are the receivers for all our intuitive information, whether we're clairsentient, clairvoyant, claircognizant, or clairaudient. Our eyes show us beauty, our tongues sense deliciousness, and our skin lets us know when we're being lovingly touched. (And the list goes on and on!) With this in mind, why wouldn't we treat our bodies like we would a loyal, beloved friend? For example, we would never tell a loyal friend something like, "I *would* love you, but you're just too fat," because we love our friends exactly as they are! They can lose weight or gain weight, get a haircut, or age twenty years, and we will love them with the same depth. We love being with them, and we love them because they are there for us—not because they win beauty contests! For our own sanity and emotional health (not to mention our magical well-being), we must begin to treat our bodies with the same amount of respect.

One wonderful way to get into this habit is by washing your body with devoted attentiveness. Whether you're in the shower or bathtub, you can choose soap or body wash that has a scent and feeling that you love, and that makes your skin feel great. Then, as you wash each body part, you can think positive, grateful, loving thoughts about that area while sending love and appreciation through your hands.

Concurrently, you might place your awareness on the healing and energizing ions generated by the moving water and envision any and all negative or challenging patterns washing away as you cleanse. You can come into the present moment and enjoy things like the feeling of the water, the scent of the soap, and the way the light filters through the window.

Simply cleansing your body in this way will take zero extra time out of the day and will reap benefits on so many levels. In addition to being physically clean, you'll be energetically cleansed and empowered, grounded in your senses and the present moment, filled with self-esteem and self-confidence, and infused with a palpable sense of the sacred. And while you might have to move through some bumps in the road when it comes to interacting with your body with presence and loving kindness, stick with the practice and the benefits will deepen and multiply over time.

Oral Hygiene

Our mouths are the place where we literally receive sustenance and vitality from the physical world. This is why, in Chinese face reading, the mouth is considered a symbol of prosperity, and the condition of the mouth dictates the quality of wealth and resources that you are drawing into your life.

When you brush your teeth in the morning, it is a good idea to do so with the intention to clear the way for abundant blessings to flow into your life experience. Think of it as a daily road-opening ritual. You might even think these words: "I now clear the way for abundant blessings and positive opportunities." Think of all that minty freshness summoning all the most delicious and sumptuous blessings into your life experience. Then, as you floss, continue thinking about clearing away any lingering blocks to your natural flow of positivity and prosperity.

Nail Care

Our hands project and receive energy. Whether you're male or female, caring for your hands and nails consciously can help refine your magical projections and your ability to receive gifts, blessings, and intuitive information. Additionally, a nice manicure can help remind you to perform your manual tasks with mindfulness and presence (so you don't get a hangnail or chip!), which in turn puts you in a mindset that is more conducive to magnetizing blessings and positive conditions.

Fashion Choices

In the past, I had trouble understanding how thinking too much about fashion could be anything other than superficial. Now, though, I feel quite differently. While I acknowledge that one can fall into the superficial trap with fashion (and many do), I also see that when employed with consciousness and intention, fashion can be a powerful magical tool. For example, as an empath, in the past I had a lot of trouble being in large crowds because I felt totally overwhelmed by all the conflicting feelings and vibes coming at me from all directions. But now, whenever I know I might be in a crowded environment (such as a concert or large festival), I choose fabric and accessories that feel both protective and soothing, such as a flowy shawl and a mirrored pendant. I then increase the magic further by empowering my fashion choices to act as protectors and buffers, helping deflect and soften all the chaotic energy and emotions.

Fashion can also be an expression of authenticity. Taking a little extra time to find and choose clothes that help you feel most like yourself can be an artform and a mode of loving communication with the humans around you. You're going to get dressed anyway, so you may as well choose your fabrics, colors, and symbols consciously, just as you would choose your materials for a charm.

Finally—and perhaps most essentially—fashion can help us get into the feeling of that which we want to experience. Since magic begins with our intention, and continues with our belief and positive expectation, we can literally shroud ourselves in colors, fabrics, styles, and symbols that help magnetize the conditions we desire. So, how do you want to feel, or what feelings will help you draw in what you want to magically create? For instance, your clothes don't have to actually be expensive, but if you feel polished and upscale in what you are wearing, you will be much more likely to magnetize wealth. So let your process of selecting your ensemble be a magical fine-tuning process. Start with your intention and then wait until you look in the mirror and something clicks and you think, "Yes! This is just right!"

The "Three Secrets Empowerment" for Clothing or Accessories

A simple way to empower a piece of clothing or an accessory with magical energy is the "three secrets empowerment," which comes from the Tibetan Black Hat tradition of feng shui, but which is actually a magical practice that is common to a number of traditions.

Before you begin, declare your intention: What brand of magical energy would you like to summon? Or, more specifically, what exactly do you want to manifest or experience? Phrase it in the present tense as if it's already true, and write it down. For example, you might write, "I am confident and articulate. I ace the interview."

The first secret is gesture. For the purpose of empowering a piece of clothing or accessory, you might choose a straightforward gesture, such as pointing a finger, or holding your open palms toward the item and visualizing magical energy streaming out of them and into the item. If you work with a wand, you might simply point the wand at the item.

The second secret is vocalization. Choose some magic words to go with your intention. They might be in English, or they might be in Sanskrit or another language that you feel spiritually and metaphysically aligned with. The important thing is that the words feel powerful for you. You might choose to simply state your intention as your vocalization ("I am confident and articulate. I ace the interview"), you might choose a mantra from your yoga practice, or you might choose to chant the name of a divinity or deity that you'd like to call on for the purpose.

The third secret is visualization. Considering your intention, plan what you will visualize, imagine, or feel. For the previous example, you might get into the feeling of confidence. You might remember a time when you felt particularly articulate, and remind yourself what it felt like. Then, you might imagine the feeling of walking out of the interview after it's over, feeling great and like you know that you did fabulously.

Standing near the item, put the three secrets together. While performing the gesture, chant your vocalization three, six, or nine times. Immediately following this, or simultaneously, employ your visualization and direct the energy that these actions have generated into the article.

Lounge Wear and Underwear

Assembling a small yet beloved lounge and underwear wardrobe (i.e., luxurious and attractive sleepwear, slippers, undies or lingerie, and robe) in which you feel divine can be a powerful magical act in and of itself. Sure, you could spend money on ingredients for five separate charms for self-esteem, prosperity, a happy home, success, and romance, or you could spend money on nice lounge wear and underwear and reap the same magical benefits…*and* be draped in luxury. Why? Well, just think of the psychological and magical ramifications of feeling fabulous under your clothes, especially during a morning or evening in. You're giving yourself the messages that you value yourself and your comfort, that you deserve luxury, that you exude the energy of success, and that you live the good life as a matter of course. You're also giving anyone you live with the message that you value their thoughts, feelings, and opinions, which can only enhance your household harmony. If you live with a partner, you're fanning the flames of attraction, and if you don't live with a partner, you're enhancing your self-esteem and feeling of receptivity and readiness for a partner (all of which help to magically draw in a partner).

Add a little focused intention to the mix, and you've got some potent magic happening, all while feeling magnificent in your cozies or intimates.

Lip Care

Remember how the mouth represents the way we draw in wealth and abundance in Chinese face reading? Well, red is a color of success, energy, and celebration. And just as painting the door to your house red can help you manifest prosperity and blessings (as per the teachings of feng shui), so can painting your mouth red with red lipstick. Similarly (and for those of you who don't wear makeup), simply keeping your lips moisturized brings in the energy of water and nourishment, and can also help keep your life and affairs in their most affluent flow—especially (you guessed it!) when you apply the lipstick or balm with the intention to activate your wealth.

Eye Care

The eyes are very magical things. Not only do they give us both subtle and overt messages about everything around us, they are also the "windows to the soul" and transmit our inner essence to the people with whom we interact. From a magical perspective, keeping them healthy, moisturized, and bright has everything to do with the way you perceive and the way you share your vision and inner essence with the world. With this in mind, it's a good idea to treat them to a good eye cream in both the morning and the evening. And, if you wear makeup, you might add intention to the process of applying it. For example, eyeliner adds a feeling of depth and authority to your appearance while helping to focus your ability to see into the heart of things. While applying it, you might think or say these words: "I own my authority. I see clearly. I know just what to do."

. . . .

As you can see, when it comes to magical self-care and interacting with your body in a loving way, the possibilities are endless. Perhaps experiment to find the methods that feel best to you, and then switch them up when you need to inject a little extra oomph into your magical routine. And, of course, remember that taking the time to take care of yourself is not selfish or extravagant: it's a necessity. And you are worth it!

Tess Whitehurst *is the author of a number of books, including* Magical Fashionista: Dress for the Life You Want, The Magic of Flowers, *and* Magical Housekeeping. *She's also a feng shui consultant and intuitive counselor. Visit her, read her blog, and sign up for her free monthly newsletter at www.tesswhitehurst.com.*

Illustrator: Kathleen Edwards

Protection Magic Manifesting in the Mundane World

Michael Furie

The idea of using magic for protection is not new, of course. Rituals and amulets designed to keep us safe from harm are older than recorded history. Some people have questioned their effectiveness, since psychic shielding or carrying an amulet won't create some kind of physical force field that could stop bullets. On the other hand, some people have asked me things like, "Since you have magical protection, why do you bother locking your doors or setting your car alarm?" Well, my answer to them is a little complicated. I *do* use magic for protection—every day, in fact. But, through several difficult life

Through several difficult life experiences, I have learned what, why, and how protection magic works, thus teaching me the very real need to take sensible mundane precautions and not rely solely on magical assistance.

experiences, I also have learned what, why, and how protection magic works, thus teaching me the very real need to take sensible mundane precautions and not rely solely on magical assistance.

I had a surprising amount of car trouble with just one vehicle. When we first got the car, it was used, so I decided to hang several protective charms from the rearview mirror and bless the car to help ensure that we would be free of problems. We had the car for four years, and in that time, we experienced several unusual emergency situations.

The first incident happened when we were driving to the birthday party of a friend. While we were on the highway, something broke loose in the manual transmission, and when we came to a stoplight, I couldn't pull it out of gear. I managed to put it into neutral, which was kind of like trying to shift through quicksand. Luckily, the car worked in all the gears, and even though it was incredibly difficult to shift, we were able to drive home and to a mechanic before finding out that something had, in the mechanic's words, "exploded in the transmission" and we shouldn't have been able to drive it at all.

The next problem came one time when we had been on the highway for about an hour. Just as we crossed into the county limits and were almost home, we stopped at a red light, and suddenly, steam began to rise from under the hood. The stoplight turned green, and I quickly pulled over to the side of the road. We called for a tow

truck, and upon arriving at the mechanic, we were told that all the water hoses had burst at once, hence the steam. The problem was solved with a simple but pricey set of new hoses.

The next bump in the road, so to speak, came a few months later when I was leaving home. I barely made it to the stop sign before the engine cut out and I had to coast to the curb. This time we found out it was a malfunctioning ignition switch. Some more money was spent and we were ready to go once again. It was at this point that my faith in my ability to work protection magic began to falter (because I wasn't paying close enough attention to the pattern), and I decided to ask for divine assistance.

For many years prior, I have been oathed to the Cailleach, the Celtic goddess of the dark half of the year. I asked her to protect us and the car. Afterward, I felt confident that we would be safe from further mishaps, but I was mistaken. Things were going pretty well until "it" happened. Okay, this was the big one, and the only reason it wasn't the final straw was thanks to divine intervention. The job I had at the time was as a field inspector for a company that gathered data for insurance underwriters. Basically, they sent me all over to diagram and photograph the houses of people who had a homeowner's insurance policy through the company.

I received a long-distance assignment well outside my usual area. It was in a little town I had never heard of, located far up in the mountains. I took two highways to get to the town nearest the base of the mountains, then took a poorly paved road that turned into a dirt-and-rock road winding up and into the mountains. The whole time I was driving up the road, I was ignoring the nagging voice in my head that was telling me to turn back. I continued deeper into the mountains and was surprised to find random cows standing in the "road" and several abandoned buildings along the way to this supposed town. For most of the journey, the road was barely wide enough for the car to fit, with a mountain on one side and a cliff on the other. The voice in my head urging me to turn back kept getting louder, but, stubbornly, I continued onward. I was smart enough to ask the Cailleach to please protect me and help me through this, at least.

Eventually I reached my destination and was shocked to find a small neighborhood with two paved roads and some very nice houses. I completed my work, and then it was time to head back down the hill. I turned around and started back, leaving the paved road and nice houses behind, and returned to the dirt, gravel, and cows. I had been driving for a while along the cliff road when I hit a huge pothole and the car skidded on the gravelly dirt and spun around. All this happened so fast, but it was one of those times when everything moved in slow motion. My life didn't flash before my eyes. Instead, there was an eerie feeling of quiet acceptance that I was going over the cliff. As the car was spinning, I hit my head on the roof, and the next thing I knew, the car was stopped. I hadn't gone over the cliff. Instead, the car was pushed up against the mountain! The way it was situated, the front of the car was pointed up. It looked like I was trying to drive straight up the mountain. I was alive and well and grateful for that, but the back end of the car was wedged in a small ditch, so even though the car miraculously started up and seemed to run fine, it was stuck.

I was miles away from the little neighborhood of houses and still several miles up in the mountains, so with little choice, I started walking. My cell phone had no service up there, and I hadn't seen a single person on the whole trip. It made more sense to try to walk down out of the mountains versus trying to walk back up to the houses, since no one was home the first time and I didn't want to trudge up the mountain. As I walked, I scanned the area, and about a mile down the road, I looked over the cliff and into the valley below. I saw a distant farmhouse, and on their property there were giant billboards painted with the words "No Shooting Domestic Pigs." I shuddered at the thought of random people showing up with guns and kept walking. As I walked, I called on the Cailleach and thanked her for slamming me against the mountain instead of letting me fall over the cliff and also asked her to help me get off the mountain. I needed to be rescued. By this time it was late afternoon, and I was certain there was no way I'd be back to the main road before dark.

I kept walking, and after another mile or so, I actually heard a vehicle approaching from behind. I was relieved, but nervous about what would appear. I couldn't believe my eyes. A silver Porsche pulled up alongside me and the driver said, "Was that your car I saw back there?" I told him it was, explaining a bit about what had happened, and he agreed to drive me to town. On the way down the mountain, he told me that he was on his way home to the San Francisco Bay area from

up north. He had gotten lost off the highway, and his GPS decided to take him through the mountain route. He ended up coming up the mountain from the other side and was following the road back down when he saw me.

The town we arrived at connected to the highway, so he got back on track and I was able to call my family and let them know what had happened and also call for a tow truck. The tow truck driver took me back up the mountain and said that he had grown up in the area and that I should have gone up the mountain from the other side, as the road was better there. Once we found the car (at around 9:00 p.m.), he said that we had driven twenty-three miles up into the mountains—that's how far I would have had to walk to get to the town. He got the car dislodged and it was drivable, so I drove it, following him on the "better" road down the north side of the mountain. Once we reached the highway, I drove back home, arriving some time around midnight.

As a result of my ill-fated journey, the rear axle of the car needed to be changed, and since I wasn't smart enough to recognize that I should have just gotten rid of the car, we bought the rear axle parts and my partner's brother changed the axle. Once that was done, I did a test drive around the block, then parked in front of his house and we went in to say our thanks and goodbyes. When we were leaving, I looked down the street and saw no cars, opened the driver's-side door, sat in the seat, reached for the door, and BOOM! The door was gone!

In the few seconds it had taken me to get in the car, another car, driving too fast and too close to the curb, had come from around the corner and slammed into my car door, bending it all the way back so it was touching the front tire. Needless to say, I was shaken, but unharmed. The car was considered totaled, so that was the end of that. Upon reflection, my experiences with that car taught me some valuable lessons about magic and how it manifests in our lives.

In believing my protection magic wasn't working because mishaps kept occurring, I was ignoring some fundamental facts: (1) if you choose to do something foolish, the Gods aren't going to stop you; and (2) even magic can't keep a bad car held together. At the time all this was occurring, I was too close to it to see the pattern of activity. Prior to the mountain crash, when the car broke down, it had happened at either the safest possible time or the car had managed to keep going until we were able to have it repaired.

When the transmission broke, for example, it shouldn't have been drivable, but it was, and therein lies the magic. When the hoses burst, when the ignition switch malfunctioned, when the front axle broke— all these things did not occur when I was driving on a bridge or fifty miles from home, or in any of the myriad ways that could have led to a serious accident. The magic protected me and helped to delay the actual breakdowns until they were the least problematic. If left to random chance, at least one of those occurrences might have happened at a terrible time. But magic cannot transform a car that's falling apart into a car that never needs a repair. You can't heal an inanimate object; it must be fixed.

The foolish actions for which I am responsible are (1) driving the car in the first place, especially since we discovered that the previous owner had raced it and it is very likely that it had suffered prior damage and wear and tear; (2) not getting consistent preventive maintenance done on it to avoid some of these problems in the first place; and (3) agreeing to that mountain town work assignment. That should have never happened. I ignored my own common sense and the nagging voice in my head telling me not to go. Since I made the conscious choice to complete the assignment, the Gods didn't interfere or stop me, presumably because I needed to learn the folly of making bad choices and also the importance of listening to my instincts.

Luckily for me, the Cailleach was there for me when I was at my most desperate. The dirt road was only one lane at best, so there really wasn't room for the car to spin once, let alone a few times. To me, the fact that I ended up stuck against the mountain instead of in the valley below was a miracle. Then being rescued by a stranger in a Porsche who "just happened" to get lost was amazing (you see why I love the Cailleach so much, right?). I think that had I not been using

protective charms and other magic, not to mention calling on the Goddess, my cliffside ordeal could have been much worse. My experiences have taught me that there is definite value in using magic for protection.

Magical Methods of Protection

I feel that it is best to use a variety of magical methods of protection to maximize the results.

SHIELDS

A good all-purpose protective measure is a classic: shielding. If you are going to use shielding for protection during travel, such as when you are driving a car, it is best to visualize a force field–type circle of energy around both yourself and the vehicle that feels like a repellent magnet, pushing away danger. In the case of driving, I would not recommend other shielding techniques such as visualizing outward-facing mirrors, since you do want to be seen by the other drivers. The force-field technique just helps to keep the other traffic from hitting you. Begin the visualization before you start the car, and see an electric-blue bubble encircle the car. Add the feeling of when you are trying to bring together the wrong ends of two magnets and they are pushing against each other. Think of any car that would veer into your lane as being magically pushed away from you. Mentally direct the force field to stay in place until you choose to disperse it, drawing energy from the universe as needed to sustain itself. Now you're all ready to go.

CHARMS

A quick, easy, and effective protective charm bag can be made from a spoonful of sea salt, a spoonful of black peppercorns, and a lock of hair or some nail clippings from the one to be protected, all tied up in a red charm bag that is then charged with protective energy. This can be carried with you to offer personal protection. Another option is to bless and charge an article of clothing as an amulet of protection. Even though it sounds a little *Wizard of* Oz, a great method is to charge your shoes so that you will be magically drawn to take the correct path and thus be protected from harm. Simply take the shoes you are going to wear and, using a wand or athame, draw a circle of energy around them. Fill this circle with electric-blue light and the desire that as long as you are wearing these shoes, you will always be on the right path. Visualize the energy and intention being absorbed into the shoes and being held there for use. Finally, open the small circle, and the shoes will be ready to wear.

Oils and Potions

A popular method of personal protection is to anoint your wrists, your third eye, and the back of your neck with any protective oil. A good blend is equal parts nettle, cinquefoil, and yarrow mixed in corn oil. If you do not like the feeling of wearing heavy oils, you can try working with a potion instead. To create a protection potion, take a tablespoon each of rosemary, peppermint, and oregano, and simmer them in two cups of water until the water is just below the boiling point. Allow the potion to cool, covered, for at least ten minutes, then strain and charge with protective energy. This potion can be used in the same manner as an oil to anoint the body or even dabbed onto the tires of a car or other objects to offer them protection. Since it is a potion made from edible ingredients, you can drink it to infuse the body with protective energy from within.

. . . .

I have learned that magic cannot and should not be relied upon as the sole source of security. In order to fully protect yourself from harm, it is very necessary to take mundane precautions, such as keeping up on preventive car maintenance and following your own intuitive common sense, along with using magic. The good news is that magic alone can be very powerful in safeguarding you from utter disaster, even if you aren't the most methodical person when it comes to security matters. For me, the bottom line for the use of protection magic is, use it, use it, use it, but also use all reasonable mundane precautions and protective measures available to you so that you are fully prepared. I see mundane effort as a facet of magical working, since all things are interconnected in the energetic sense. To then leave my car alarm off would be to leave a gap in the fullness of my protective efforts. To my mind, this would be like leaving an opening in a magic circle—a hole in the ozone layer, so to speak—that would only serve to invite trouble. I hope that my strange tale of car troubles has helped to show that even when we may not realize it, and though perhaps not as we originally intended, our magic is always working on our behalf.

Michael Furie (*Northern California*) *is the author of* Spellcasting for Beginners *and* Supermarket Magic, *both published by Llewellyn, and has been a practicing Witch for over eighteen years. He began studying Witchcraft at age twelve and at the age of seventeen officially took the oaths of the Craft. An American Witch, he practices in the Irish tradition and is a priest of the Cailleach. You can find him online at www.michaelfurie.com.*

Illustrator: Rik Olson

Taking Advantage of
Life's Little Daily Oracles

Barbara Ardinger

From the I Ching and the Tarot to runes and angel cards, we modern Pagans love our oracular tools. We scry and dowse. Some of us observe the flights of birds, converse with bees, and listen to the whispers of the leaves on the trees. Many of us draw a card or a rune every morning to see what the day might bring. I used to do that, too, but it got to be too much trouble (and, well, I got bored), so now I pay more attention to the little daily oracles I find. Sometimes they tell me what the day might hold for me.

Fortune Cookies

What are little daily oracles? Maybe not the things you'd expect. Let's start with the wise sayings that come in fortune cookies. I don't eat the cookies, but I save the fortunes. And I don't just throw them in a drawer. Sometimes I tuck them in my wallet or in a book. The two that have been under the checks in my checkbook for maybe twenty years say, *Fortune truly helps those who are of good judgment* and *Success and wealth are in your fate*. Thank you, Peking Noodle Company. The former, of course, is just good common sense; the latter cheers me up on days when I'm feeling impoverished—which happens a lot less often than it used to. Who knows? Maybe the Peking Noodle Company is on to something! Has anyone used those mysterious numbers they give us to win the lottery?

When I moved into this apartment a few years ago, I sorted through my fortune cookie collection and taped a couple dozen of them to the kitchen cabinet where I stand when I butter my morning toast. Now I make it a practice to glance up at them every morning. Whatever my gaze alights on gives me something to ponder. *Someone is speaking well of you*. That's good. Who is it? What are they saying? Will I get a phone call from an old friend today? Will a new author send me his book to edit today? *You have a talent for all that is artistic*. Even though I once drew a magnificent contour drawing of a brussels sprout, I'm not a visual artist. But I'm good with words and I'm nothing if not creative. It's very comforting to have this talent affirmed in the morning.

However...

The folly of mistaking a paradox for a discovery, a metaphor for a proof, a torrent of verbiage for a spring of capital truth, and oneself for an oracle, is inborn in us.

—Paul Valéry, *Introduction to the Method of Leonardo da Vinci*

Some days, my eyes stop on this fortune: *Forget all that wishful thinking and be practical.* That's certainly good advice. It makes me think of that splendid bumper sticker, Ask the Goddess, then do your homework.

We Pagans know that we cannot just stare and stare at, say, a necklace in a jewelry store window and expect it to suddenly fly out and land around our neck. The true magic lies in our intention (always heeding the Wiccan Rede, "Harm none") and the workings we do, whether in circle or at home, as we work magic in our imagination. No, we cannot in fact run our lives by fortune cookies, but like a good reading with Tarot cards or runes, we can get a glimpse of what might happen and what potentials lie in our path. But it's up to us to get the hint and do the work.

One of my most recent fortune cookies said, *You will soon witness a miracle.* Let's not scoff. Something miraculous happens every day. The earth keeps turning. Leaves and flowers return in the spring. Birds fly and sing. On a more mundane level, the car starts or we don't get run over by that big Mercedes speeding down the street. We wander into a shop and find exactly what we want and it's on sale. The cat strolls up and starts purring. We who write books receive a royalty statement from Amazon. We don't need saintly apparitions approved by any church to run our lives. I think the little miracles are more useful than the big ones. Suppose you receive this fortune cookie about a miracle…what will you do?

I'm sure you've learned, as I have, to be cautious about divination. Though the Muggles want to know the future as fervently as anyone else, they scoff at our "superstitions." Then they plunk down their silver and get a reading. As we know (or certainly should know), our large and small oracles are not absolute predictors of absolute truth about the absolute future. No, they predict possibilities. They comment gnomically on the present and ambiguously on the future. We need, of course, to avoid creating self-fulfilling prophecies and fantasies by staying grounded.

Let's just pay attention to every day of our lives. Pay attention and see what happens.

Bibliomancy

Another little daily oracle may rise out of the morning paper or the book you're currently reading. This is called bibliomancy. In the olden days, a seeker would open the Bible at random and take the first verse he saw as God's Inerrant Advice. (I wish they'd all, every one of them, open their Bibles more often to Matthew 5–7, the Sermon on the Mount: "Blessed are they…," "Judge not, that ye be not judged.")

Here's how bibliomancy works. Pick up your morning paper. Close your eyes and shuffle through the pages until one feels right. (You know the feeling.) With eyes still closed, poke at the paper. Open your eyes and read the sentence under or near your finger. Read it out of context of the news story (or ad) and consider it. Is there any application to your life? Or pick up the book you read at lunch. I'm currently reading a history of the Tudor dynasty in England (Henry VII to Elizabeth I). Here's what I just now got: "...he easily established himself as the leading practitioner of his dubious trade." The context is about one of William Cecil's spies, but that doesn't matter to bibliomancy. What this sentence might mean in my life today is that I need to be careful if I receive a phone call or an e-mail soliciting money for some cause or other. Or maybe someone who comes to my door will be someone I shouldn't listen to. Or maybe I should be more careful in my editing today. The day's not over yet, but I hope you agree that it's good to be prepared. Try bibliomancy for yourself.

Logomancy

We could also get a glimpse of the day's proceedings from what we might call logomancy (or maybe I should call it babelmancy). This is when we overhear a conversation, say, at our neighbor's door, in the elevator at work, or words drifting across the office. Do not eavesdrop. Just be alert for words or phrases that seem to go *ding, ding, ding!* in your head. Again, context doesn't matter, and don't be self-absorbed or paranoid. When people are talking, they're not necessarily talking about you. Just pick up the words or a phrase that might tell you something you need to know. Logomancy can also work with morning TV shows and drive-time talk radio. We hardly ever pay 100 percent attention to the TV or radio anyway, but sometimes there's something that jumps out and gets our attention. Consider what you're hearing. It might mean something.

Jiffy Numerology

Numerology is another useful tool. We calculate the numbers in the address of the house we're looking at. Will it be propitious to live there? We calculate our new phone number. We calculate the VIN or license plate number of our new car. If you're not familiar with numerology, either get a good book on the topic or look for helpful websites or even apps that explain what the basic digits (1–9) mean, plus the master numbers. (Take a look at www.astrology-numerology .com/numerology.html.)

I have a friend who does what I call jiffy numerology on the serial number of the first dollar bill she receives as change on any given day. I bet jiffy numerology also works with bigger bills. Here's what a twenty dollar bill I just pulled out of my wallet says: IA73045150A. This equals $9 + 1 + 7 + 3 + 0 + 4 + 5 + 1 + 5 + 0 + 1 = 36$, which reduces to 9, which indicates the end of a cycle. It probably means I'm gonna spend that bill (and then I can do jiffy numerology on the change).

I also know people who do jiffy numerology on the license plate numbers of cars in front of them while they're stuck in traffic. Or they make up words using the letters on the plate. You have to be able to add in your head, of course, but isn't that good mental exercise? (I live in California, where we have long license plate numbers.) Let's say the car in front of you says: 6MCS7782, or $6 + 4 + 3 + 1 + 7 + 7 + 8 + 2 = 38$, which reduces to 11, the master number of communication. Are you going to give a speech today? Write a report? Or an article for *Llewellyn's 2015 Witches' Companion*? ($2015 = 8 =$ power. Whoopee!)

Daily Walk

Finally, if you take a daily walk, see what your route tells you. I live in a good urban neighborhood and walk on sidewalks past houses in a wide variety of architectural styles. No matter which of my half-dozen regular routes I take, I always walk in the sunwise direction so I'm winding things forward, not unwinding them. When I see a cat, I consider that a tiny bit of good luck. When I meet someone, I say hi, and they usually say hi back to me. More good fortune. When I see a penny, I always pick it up and tuck it in my pocket as I say out loud, "For those in need." That night, I put the penny on my Dame Fortuna altar.

As you walk, what signals do you get from the universe or the Goddess that might mean something in your life? A cooling breeze? Does that mean you need to cool down about some situation in your life? Are you too windy? A chirpy bird talking to you? What is it saying? As always, pay attention.

· · · · · · · · · · · · ·

What can you learn from life's little daily oracles? The little oracles may not give us the famous Big Picture that a natal astrological chart or full Tarot reading might, but I believe it's good to get hints of how my life may go just for today. Tomorrow, I'll check out tomorrow's little daily oracles. Try it for yourself. Invent new little daily oracles for yourself and tell your friends about them.

Barbara Ardinger, PhD (*www.barbaraardinger.com and www.facebook .com/barbara.ardinger*), *is the author of* Secret Lives, *a novel about crones and other magical folks, and* Pagan Every Day, *a unique daybook of daily meditations. Her other books include* Goddess Meditations (*the first-ever book of meditations focusing on goddesses*), Finding New Goddesses (*a parody of goddess encyclopedias*), *and an earlier novel,* Quicksilver Moon (*which is realistic... except for the vampire*). *Her monthly blogs appear on her website and on* Feminism and Religion, *feminismandreligion.com, where she is one of three regular Pagan contributors. Barbara lives in Long Beach, California, with her two rescued Maine coon cats, Schroedinger and Heisenberg.*

Illustrator: Tim Foley

Interpreting Omens: When a Black Cat Crosses Your Path, Does It Mean a Darn Thing?

Diana Rajchel

L ife's chaos came on strong during a recent Mercury retrograde with its attached supermoon. Some young men assaulted my sweetie during his weekend run. A few days later, we discovered I needed surgery—pronto. The very next day, my sweetie totaled the car we shared, leaving us without transportation to the hospital. Our pool of friends helped us work that out, but then a four-day blackout and a cluster of problems with a car rental left us to lease a car under duress.

Small, weird incidents happened at the time, too. A woman accosted me for taking a picture of a flower. Three unrelated people, all of whom I had no interest in reconnecting with, contacted me on the same day. An intern I had struggled to train quit just as she found a work rhythm. The onslaught left me confused, looking for meaning in the extreme string of events weaving through our lives.

The calm night came as an oasis from the craziness. As roses bloomed and heat kissed our skin, my sweetie and I made our nighttime rounds of our neighborhood. It felt nice to do something as banal as go for a walk. We paused at our favorite places—the park with the glowing sculptures, the bridge over the drainage field—and then strolled by the quirky houses that mixed Wild West with Great White North. While I took in the big picture, my partner looked at the details that blurred past him on his daily runs. One detail jumped out at him.

He paused midstep. "Oh hey! Froggie!" A toad sat squarely in our path, at the edge of a cement driveway. As we paused to inspect it, the

toad hopped away, almost hitting the edge of my partner's sneakers. At a perfect 180-degree angle, a beetle the size of a half dollar scuttled away from the toad.

I felt a tingle across the top of my feet. It made me want to step out of the line we were about to cross. I knew my sweetie would argue with me about it—going two blocks out of our way to avoid a beetle and a frog. After the cascade of prior events, my paranoia was a natural but still-to-be-questioned reaction. I stepped through, keeping my misgivings to myself.

A toad and a beetle right in our way had all the marks of an omen. It also had all the marks of a little kid playing. I did not need life to get any weirder. My visceral reaction told me that the creatures' appearance meant something. I hoped it meant something minor.

My last encounter with a toad had turned into a bad omen because I was careless. I mistook one for a rock while cleaning stones out of my garden. When one "stone" blinked at me, I threw it in surprise. I probably hurt it. Upon looking up the meaning later, I found out that killing a toad guarantees bad luck.

I don't live in that home anymore. It was sold to new owners who raised the rent two months later. That only started the downslide of an exceptionally difficult year. Now, a toad in my path gave me pause.

I worry enough when omens appear to me. Omens appearing to my skeptical partner worry me beyond reason. I wondered, why wasn't this toad eating this beetle?

As I observed, time seemed to slow. The tingle across the top of my feet increased. I stood on the edge of a secret border: frog and beetle on one side, me on the other. I did not sense the revulsion I normally do for most six-legged creatures. All of this happened at twilight.

Indeed, we had encountered an omen.

I had no way of knowing whether what I saw was good or bad. I just knew it *meant something*.

Interpreting Omens

Omens are tricky to interpret, especially in North America, where ancestries merge and blur. We do look to animal behavior, to wind direction, to folklore, to divine meaning. Yet one cultural influence may negate the symbolic meaning of another.

Dream dictionaries, founded on Western concepts, can help. While rarely useful in defining dreams, they are often stunningly accurate when interpreting omens in waking life.

On the way home, I looked up the meaning of the toad on my phone. The toad, according to that dictionary, indicates closeted feelings. I sought a second opinion in a different dream dictionary at home. This source suggested a tendency to hide from beauty.

All sources defined the beetle as a warning. Most beetles represent destructive forces at work. I was ready to receive the warning after all the disasters but felt at a loss as to what else to do. One dictionary made a caveat for scarab beetles, but as far as I knew, scarabs did not exist in Minnesota. Then I looked up this beetle: the Minnesota dung beetle, relative to the famed scarab.

Two dubious symbols had literally crossed our path. The meaning did not lie in the creatures alone, but in their behavior. Although it had seemed that they wanted us to see them, they had bailed off our path as fast as possible.

It takes practice to recognize and read omens. Human beings are most inclined toward omen reading during times of stress—and times of stress are when we are most likely to misinterpret them. It helps to look for certain physical hallmarks. When you observe the phenomena, do you get a sense of time slowing down? Does the scene draw your attention away from your surroundings? Is the behavior of what you observed typical? Maybe something you noticed but thought trivial keeps popping up in your mind later. All these indicate a possible omen.

> **It takes practice to recognize and read omens. Human beings are most inclined toward omen reading during times of stress—and times of stress are when we are most likely to misinterpret them.**

The only way to know is to consider what you saw and see how its symbolism fits with what is already going on in your life.

Omens often appear simply because you asked. If you requested a sign relating to a concern, the omens encountered communicate with you.

Omens can happen indoors or out, with animals, insects, objects, or people. As long as it has meaning to you, it has meaning as an omen. For example, once as I walked down my apartment hallway, I saw a cat that looked like it had clawed its way out of a Stephen King novel stalking the hallway. It paused at each doorway to scratch and yowl. No doors opened. Who in their right mind would let that thing in their home? A neighbor passed me in the hallway and asked, "Is that cat yours?"

"No, that thing is not my doing." The odd words from my own mouth surprised me. That casual exchange between neighbors had the slowed-time effect of an omen. I later looked up "cat" in a dream dictionary. Per that source, a cat yowling meant someone was speaking ill of me to anyone who might listen. The reactions from my neighbors—both the one in the hall and the ones who did not let that cat in—told me that the results of these people's efforts would be unsuccessful.

The scary cat only started that particular conversation. A few days later, on a walk in the woods, I encountered a raccoon pacing back and forth and hissing. This signified that the rumor-mongering continued. As I progressed on my walk, I saw an owl watching me. It was a message from Athena: she observed and was taking my side. Greater wisdom would prevail.

The trickiest omens to interpret are those that use human beings as the symbolic messages. Some strange encounters are just people acting out their foibles and symptoms. Some are not. Mythology is rife with stories of gods and ancestors that venture out among mortals in disguise. The man in the three-piece suit skateboarding down the center line of city traffic might be an entry-level employee getting his kicks. Or he might be Hermes, signaling an incoming message. The gods have modern interests, and that interest includes you.

Once, when I walking to work downtown, a man stopped me on the street to ask me directions to the nearest post office. He wore a gray suit and a top hat and held a cane he did not use. "May I comment on your appearance?" he asked. I said, "Sure," hoping this wouldn't turn into a diet advertisement. He looked me up and down. "Very casual."

I had spent the night before fretting over whether my outfit suited my bank job. The encounter showed all the signs of an omen. Time slowed—I have no memory of anything that went on in the background, despite this man stopping me on a busy city street. He asked a question about a message delivery service.

You can also figure out omens with nonlinear journaling and divination. You can confirm or deny an incident by asking Tarot cards or runes, "Did X event mean something?" Using a journal, write down incidents that concern you on the edges of a page. In the center, free-associate; write down any small but striking incidents that come to mind. Symbols may pop out at you—your subconscious noticed, even if you didn't.

A walk around the block can expose all sorts of messages. Some are warnings, such as the person yelling rude things while driving by, or the playground you pass where one child bullies others as the bully's mother looks on, doing nothing. But others are good tidings, like finding a scarab beetle or seeing the clouds parting from the sun. If you happen to believe that nature is God manifest, then omen reading is an ideal way to have a face-to-face conversation. Go be in it and see what the arrangements say to you.

Recommended Reading and Apps

Dream Sight: a Dictionary for Interpreting Any Dream by Dr. Michael Lennox. Woodbury, MN: Llewellyn, 2011.

Dream Moods, http://www.dreammoods.com. This is also available as a smartphone app, with an exhaustive review of dream symbolism.

DreamForth. This is another smartphone app, which looks at dreams in thematic passages.

Diana Rajchel *lives in northeast Minneapolis with her life partner. She is the author of the book* Divorcing a Real Witch *and the executive editor for the* Pagan Newswire Collective.

Illustrator: Christa Marquez

Witchcraft Essentials

PRACTICES, RITUALS & SPELLS

Planning a Wiccan Wedding

Deborah Lipp

As of this writing, I'm a few short weeks away from my wedding, so the subject of wedding planning is not abstract to me. Naturally I'm thrilled. I'm also kind of a wreck. Wedding planners and other professionals who deal with weddings will tell you that stress and nerves are normal, so build in extra time to your schedule as a cushion. That way, when you get to the point where you're a wreck like me, you can also breathe a sigh of relief that everything is already pretty much in order.

The fact that your wedding is Wiccan or Pagan shouldn't add additional stress, but it may raise additional questions for you. If I could do an infographic instead of an article, that might actually be helpful, because the best way to go about this is via a decision tree. Each answer leads to the next question, and ultimately to the result: the Wiccan wedding of your dreams.

Decision 1: Wiccan or Wiccan-Flavored?

Are you, in fact, having a full-blown Wiccan or Pagan ritual, or are you infusing a more conventional or non-denominational wedding with Wiccan or Pagan elements?

You are unlikely to need my help answering this one, because you already know. Most people, I think, have a gut response to the question, either "Hell NO, I'm not casting a circle in front of Uncle Joe!" or "Damn RIGHT it's going to be a circle: my wedding, my religion!" You already know how far out of the broom closet you are, and that's how most people make this decision.

Decision 2: How Big a Ceremony?

Again, you're not reading this article for help in making this decision. People decide on the size of their wedding based on lots of factors, but primarily how big the families are, what the available budget is, and what kind of event really feels right.

Whether you're having a Wiccan ceremony or another kind of ceremony with a Wiccan flavor—indeed, *regardless* of what kind of ceremony—the number of people makes the greatest difference in how any ceremony is created. Whether the subject is marriage or a full moon, Summer Solstice or Coming of Age, everything in ritual planning hinges upon the number of people. It changes everything from physical blocking to acoustics, so it's really the first essential decision.

Of course, if you have already looked into booking a venue, hiring a caterer, buying booze, or whatever else has gone into your wedding planning, you quickly realized that headcount was incredibly important.

Decision 3: To Handfast or Not to Handfast?

Handfasting originally was a Scottish betrothal, until Sir Walter Scott reimagined it in 1820 as a temporary marriage, lasting a year and a day. Many Pagans today use this latter meaning and make a distinction between contracted, temporary handfasting and lifelong, legal marriage. Other Pagans use "handfasting" simply to mean "Pagan wedding."

If you choose to use this word to refer to your own wedding, you'll undoubtedly want to incorporate the physical handfasting—the tying of the couple's hands together with a cord. (Usually it's the wrists, not hands, that are bound.)

There's a lot of variation in the cord itself. Some people use a single cord of a symbolic color (often red), and some people use a braid; again, the colors could be symbolic. Some people tie the hands together and then untie them at some point in the ritual. Others leave

them tied—there is even a custom of having the couple consummate their union while still bound hand to hand. Others wrap the cords and do not tie. All of these have symbolic meaning and can be elaborated on in spoken words used around the act of fasting the hands: Are you "tied" together, or connected yet free? Are the bonds still present when the cords are removed? Talking about these ideas will beautify and personalize the experience.

Keep in mind that there's a pragmatic component here. If you're leaving the hands tied together, then the exchange of rings has to come first. If you're untying the hands, you shouldn't use elaborate knots that might get stuck in the middle of things.

Decision 4: Indoors or Outdoors?

An outdoor ceremony is beautiful, but consider: Will your candles stay lit? Do you want torches for quarters? Do you want to provide shade? Will people be wearing ritual robes, medieval garb, or street clothes? If you've chosen street clothes (my guests will be in cocktail attire), make sure the women know that you'll be outdoors, so they don't wear heels that will sink into the earth!

On the other hand, if you're at a rented indoor venue (as opposed to someone's home), make sure you understand what the rules are. Open flames and water sprinkled on the floor, for example, are two things that a catering hall might not allow.

So, based on these four decisions, we'll look at four types of ceremonies.

Wiccan Rituals

When I teach ritual creation, I emphasize that you should start with a basic outline that works for all your rites. I have a "regular Pagan script" that I use (an example appears in my book *The Elements of Ritual*). Whenever there's occasion to write a new script—a holiday celebration, a lunar eclipse, a rite of passage—I just take my standard script and modify it. This has a number of advantages. As a Priestess,

I already know what I'm doing and have the steps memorized. The script already works structurally, it already makes theological sense, and I know exactly where to insert changes. Basically, it's a template.

Whatever the reason I'm modifying my script, I'm going to look at specific spots: the welcome statement, the invocations, and the quarter-callings. Then there's the vast ritual area after the quarters are called and before Cakes and Wine, which is where most "special occasion" ritual goes. This is because ritual behavior raises energy, and that energy culminates in the Cakes and Wine, which become imbued with the blessing of the magic that preceded it (all of this is discussed in exhaustive detail in *The Elements of Ritual*).

Changes might also be made to Cakes and Wine itself, and will certainly be made to closing statements that come after Cakes and Wine, quarter farewells, and the formal end of the ritual.

I would advise the structure to be something like this:

1. Cast circle and call quarters as usual (with changes to the wording).

2. Invoke the Gods in a manner specific to the occasion.

3. Bring in the wedding party and perform the marriage.

4. Have the couple perform Cakes and Wine as their first marital act.

5. Have the couple leave the circle by jumping a broom.

6. Thank the Gods, thank the quarters.

7. Close the circle as usual.

There are a lot of handfasting scripts floating around on the Internet to inspire you. Two excellent ones appear in *Magical Rites from the Crystal Well* by Ed Fitch and *A Witches' Bible: The Complete Witches' Handbook* by Janet and Stewart Farrar.

Who Is Attending?

The first thing you want to look at is, will anyone unfamiliar with Wicca be attending? If so, there are key spots where a little explanation is called for.

One of the basics of ritual creation is to have a clear-cut beginning and ending. The "welcome" statement at the beginning of an ordinary Wiccan circle can be very brief, but this is a good time to give a little speech to the guests. What's included is up to you. I like to make sure that something about the sacredness of love is present, perhaps quoting the Charge by saying something like, "In our tradition, we believe that 'all acts of love and pleasure' are rituals, and so this is the most sacred of occasions." A simple explanation of what is to follow might include, "We will use our ritual tools to make this place holy," and "We will seal a circle around our rite to contain the magic of love."

Some people who ordinarily use swords and athames in their rituals choose to use wands and staffs when non-Pagans are present, so that knives don't frighten anyone. If there are small children about— flower girls and ring bearers included—you want to make sure any blades are secure.

A Word about Polarity

Polarity is considered a core concept of traditional Wiccan ritual and theology. It is the idea that reality is a binary of This/Not This, such as dark/light, positive/negative, day/night, or yin/yang. Often it is expressed as a gender binary: male/female, God/Goddess. The power derived from bringing together poles is found in chemistry, electrical engineering, and magic.

Same-sex couples may find a handfasting ceremony based around gender polarity to be unsuitable. You might eliminate polarity entirely, working a more generally Pagan rite that doesn't include the concept. Or you might adjust the ritual script so that a polar energetic interplay remains but isn't described heterosexually. My partner and I started creating our handfasting from a script that included an invocation of paired gods and goddesses from a variety of cultures: Shiva and Parvati, Jove and Juno, Ishtar and Tammuz, and so forth. We kept the polarity present throughout the rite, but eliminated this and other heteronormative references.

Option 1: A Small Wiccan Ritual

This is probably where most people end up: fewer than fifty people in a traditional ritual made up of other Wiccans or Pagans, perhaps in addition to a more conventional wedding "for the family."

As mentioned earlier, start with a familiar baseline for your ritual. If you have a standard rite you use, modify it rather than starting from scratch. You'll feel more comfortable.

A small ceremony allows for a lot more group participation. For example, you might pass the handfasting cords around (if you've decided to use them) to each person attending, asking people to send energy into them prior to the binding. This isn't practical if more than about twenty people are in attendance. You might have everyone bring a flower to add to the bride's bouquet or to place on the altar, or candles of love and unity might be passed.

A smaller group is likely to be more cohesive as well. Singing together will be effective in a small group, while a larger group is unlikely to all know the same songs and chants.

Finally, the small group is likely to be more informal. This is where the couple might get away with sneaking off somewhere to consummate their marriage after jumping the broom and while the circle is still going on. There's no way you can get away with it in a big crowd!

Option 2: A Larger Wiccan Ritual

Once you have more than about fifty people, the intimacy of doing things together will be too time-consuming and will make your wedding guests restless. Instead of passing things around, use verbal call-and-response and group working.

For example, with twenty people, you can pass the handfasting cords. With ninety, the High Priestess or High Priest can simply ask the guests to send their energy into the cords while holding them up high so all can see. Similarly, ask the crowd to verbally agree that they will lend their love and support to the marriage (they'll all holler "I do!," which will be very gratifying).

While a small group might all know the same song, a large group is better off with a shared "om" or tone.

Speed is of the essence with a larger group. Don't race to the finish, but don't linger over ritual elements that are optional and pretty. You have to expect a variety of attention spans among your attendees. A circle-casting is a longer beginning, before getting to the main event, than, say, a church service, so padding it with a lot of extra readings is not a great idea.

People tend to become observers rather than participants in a larger crowd, so giving them responses to speak is great. Avoiding having your guests sit and watch for over an hour is also great.

Wiccan-Flavored Ceremonies

For many betrothed people, a Wiccan ritual is just not an option, or it's only an option as a separate, private affair in addition to the more customary to-do. You may be feeling kind of stuck with your non-Wiccan wedding, or you may be happy with the choice. Your non-Wiccan wedding may be a joyful compromise between you and your future spouse, or it may be a begrudging appeasement to your family, or something entirely different. Whatever the reason, the trick is to infuse the ceremony with things that feel good to you, and that make it feel more like your spiritual "home."

Your non-Wiccan wedding may be a joyful compromise between you and your future spouse, or it may be a begrudging appeasement to your family, or something entirely different.

In writing this, I am assuming that you are in the broom closet, and the ceremony isn't Wiccan for that reason. This might not be true. If you are open about your religion, you will have a wider variety of options than those I'm about to proffer. The rest of this article presents ways of incorporating a Wiccan flavor discreetly into a ceremony, in such a way as to prevent your guests from understanding these elements are Pagan while still going a long way toward satisfying your own Pagan soul.

Can the Gods be made present in your ceremony? Discreet references to Mother Nature, to the light of the Sun and Moon, to the protective blanket of the Sky, can potentially be worked into homilies or be present in carefully selected readings.

Readings in general give you the opportunity to select Craft-related poetry or statements. Ed Fitch (cited earlier) has several beautiful readings in his handfasting ceremony, one of which I read (slightly edited) at one of my sisters' weddings. Pieces that you have used in ritual can be meaningful to you while not alarming your guests.

Unity ceremonies are trendy now—people use candles, sand, salt, corn, or wine, blending two separate things into one, to symbolize the uniting of lives and families. You can easily incorporate something like this in a way that reflects your Pagan values. Because of this trend, wedding guests have become accustomed to the introduction of additional ritual elements into ceremonies that are otherwise conventional.

Handfasting itself is not out of the question, especially if you have Celtic heritage. You can explain it as an old Celtic marriage custom.

The four elements (or five, if that's how you work) can be incorporated into your ceremony as well, and would not be jarring. Earth, Air, Fire, and Water are so much a part of Western heritage that it will sound, even to the uninitiated, completely ordinary or a little New Agey.

Finally, you may be able to imbue your wedding ceremony with steps from Wiccan ritual that can be pulled out of context—because sometimes, context is universal. For example, asking your guests to close their eyes and visualize is both universal and very Pagan.

OPTION 3: A SMALL WICCAN-FLAVORED CEREMONY

If you're having a small wedding, you have a lot of choices. Your wedding guests are likely to expect a certain level of informality, and this gives you freedom to add things that may seem quirky or offbeat to your guests, but that spell "Wicca" for you. This is especially true if the wedding is non-denominational.

With fewer than thirty in attendance, you can consider having your guests form a circle. My aunt and uncle were married in 1974 or so. The ceremony was performed by a Unitarian-Universalist minister and was decidedly hippie-flavored. We stood in a circle. My aunt and uncle are not Pagan, but a circle felt loving and inclusive to them.

With a small ceremony, you can easily have everyone participate. If you're binding hands, you can pass the cord around, just as you might in a Wiccan ceremony. A candle or another object can be passed around instead, and doing something like this can come with an explanation that is not specifically religious but speaks to your spiritual values. Asking people to lend their personal energy is, after all, a very Wiccan thing to do, while not being alien to people of other faiths.

Another way to get people to participate is to have each guest bring something into the ceremony—perhaps something that was on their chair, or in their program, when they arrived. Each guest could add a flower to the altar, or a crystal, coming up one at a time to contribute their piece of the wedding ceremony. You might even have four different kinds of tokens distributed to guests, one for each of the four elements.

Here's how it might work: The officiant could say something like, "We'd like to bring the energy of Air to this marriage, so that it's breezy and thoughtful. Would any guest who received a feather in their program bring it to the altar now?" Then wait for those people to step forward. Then, when they return to their places, do the same for Fire with a small candle or a piece of amber, Water with a sea-shell, and Earth with a stone.

Remember that a small ceremony comes with fewer expectations and a lot more freedom, just because it's small. You can leverage this to infuse it with Wiccan components that do not scream "Witchcraft!" at your guests.

OPTION 4: A LARGER WICCAN-FLAVORED CEREMONY

A larger wedding can be the hardest ceremony to personalize. Once you've got more than fifty people (which isn't even big, as weddings go—I'm having more than a hundred), it will be almost impossible to include things like passing an object or standing in a circle. In this case, you will have to rely on moments that can be shared by everyone at once. A group this size will primarily watch and listen.

What about a grounding and centering? Everyone will be seated, the ceremony is about to begin, and you could, at this point, ask people to calm themselves, be fully present, and bring their loving attention to this very important moment.

Music is traditional in a wedding, and the choice of music is a way that many people make the experience more meaningful. You can choose music with a Pagan theme, or that you've used in past rituals.

As a Pagan, you are probably deeply connected to the magical and spiritual power of community. As such, you probably already understand that part of the meaning of a wedding is its shared nature. Maybe this is why you've chosen to have a big ceremony. At its best, community anchors our rites of passage and holds us accountable to our commitments and growth. It is, then, very Pagan (although not *exclusively* Pagan) to ask your wedding guests to do this: to hold you, the newlyweds, in their loving embrace, to lend their personal energy and support to this life change. Word the question in a way that reflects your values, and have the guests, as a group, say "I do" or "We do" to support your intention.

Readings are the most common way to personalize a large wedding, since everyone is listening at once. You can choose from a variety of sources that may be explicitly Pagan, and may even be ritual passages that you've used in other contexts. You can also select from mythological sources, the works of writers and poets you admire, Buddhism, Hinduism, and so forth. With readings, the world is at your feet, and the hard part is narrowing it down! Unless they're very short, more than three or four readings will make your guests restless, but a small number of carefully selected passages can go a long way toward incorporating your spirituality into the ceremony.

Finally, consider imagery. Wicca and Paganism are replete with visual and tactile images, from gods and goddesses, to elemental representatives, to gems and herbs. You may choose to be totally stealth about your path and still incorporate these images into your décor, your color scheme, your favors, and more. Even your cake and/or cake topper can represent Wicca in some way.

Star-shaped confetti on the tables may say "sparkle" to your guests but "pentagram" to you. Herb bundles as centerpieces are aromatic as well as witchy. A gold and silver color scheme can be your way of representing the marriage of Sun and Moon, or brown and green can represent Mother Earth. I decorated my gift card box in accordance with my witchy theme.

· · · · · · · · · · · · ·

It's easy to get caught up in the Wedding Industrial Complex, with all the things you "should" do or "everyone" does. But however large or small your wedding, you don't have to do it "their" way. The idea is to create a ceremony and celebration that reflects who you are as a couple. Maybe that means a handfasting circle, and maybe it doesn't. Maybe it means five of your closest friends, and maybe it means two hundred. Regardless of your choices, there are many steps within the experience where you can stop and say, This is something I can reshape and make it mine.

May the Gods bless your marriage. May your love for each other reflect the love of the Gods.

Deborah Lipp *is the author of six books, including* Merry Meet Again: Lessons, Life & Love on the Path of a Wiccan High Priestess *and* The Elements of Ritual: Air, Fire, Water and Earth in the Wiccan Circle. *Deborah has been Wiccan for over thirty years, and a High Priestess of the Gardnerian tradition since 1986. She's been published in* newWitch, Llewellyn's Magical Almanac, Pangaia, *and* Green Egg. *Deborah is also an avid media writer and blogger, and is co-owner of* Basket of Kisses: Smart Discussion About Smart Television (*www.lippsisters .com*). *She lives in Rockland County, NY, with her spouse, Melissa.*

Illustrator: Bri Hermanson

Magical Visualization

James Kambos

Conceive it. Believe in it. Receive it!

These are the three steps I use when I perform any type of magical visualization for spellcasting or any other related magical work. Basically, magical visualization involves seeing a goal or desire in your mind's eye, concentrating on it, then willing your desire to become a physical reality in your life. Words of Power may or may not accompany your visualization.

Magical visualization is the cornerstone of all magic. Without it, the results of our magical work would be haphazard at best. Almost every magical act, spell, or ritual involves some type of visualization and then following through with the necessary steps to bring about the desired effects.

Almost every magical act, spell, or ritual involves some type of visualization and then following through with the necessary steps to bring about the desired effects.

Magical visualization, also known as creative visualization, is as old as magic itself. Think about the ancient artwork found in prehistoric cave dwellings. Much of this art depicts hunting scenes, showing our early ancestors in the various stages of a successful hunt. This art wasn't just for recording their activities or for pleasure. The art they created in this instance was part of their visualization technique used to reach a goal.

They conceived a need, which in this case was that they needed food. This was their goal. Then they believed that they'd be able to achieve this goal. That's obvious because their art showed them successfully tracking and killing wild game. Lastly, they received it. They went hunting after being inspired by the visualizations they created, and, knowing they could do it, they brought home the game they hunted. After taking action according to their visualizations, they were able to feed their clan. Did they realize they were practicing a form of magical visualization? Probably not. To them, it was just part of a very natural process. To ancient people, the act of magical visualization was instinctive.

Today, most of us—Witch and non-Witch—live grounded in the physical world, or the world of form. This is our reality. To most of us, this is the *only* plane of existence. This is easy to understand; the physical world is where we live our day-to-day lives. Unlike the ancients, such as the cave dwellers I've mentioned, we are far removed from our magical roots. The very idea that we could wish for something, believe it could happen, and then have it come true is a hard concept for many of us to accept. And to some, it's even a bit scary. But ancient humans didn't have these hang-ups. They realized that magical visualization wasn't a supernatural power. They knew instead that it was very natural and that everyone could benefit from it.

The act of magical visualization isn't always easy. It can take practice, especially in our high-speed world where we are bombarded with an excess of visual stimulation. But with some of the tips and techniques I'll share with you, you'll be able to focus on your visualizations more clearly and easily. This will help you get the desired results from your magical work.

Keep in mind that you don't need to be a genius to perform magical visualization, nor does it require psychic abilities. All it takes is will and the ability to focus.

The Basic Steps of Magical Visualization

Now let me explain in a little more detail the basic steps of magical visualization, and how the process works from start to finish.

Conceive

This is where it all begins. You must conceive an idea of what it is you need. At this early stage, whatever it is you're seeking is already on its way to you. This is because your thought, vision, or idea is taking shape in the Unseen Realm. Earlier, when I said we are far removed from our magical roots, this is what I was thinking of. As centuries have passed, the human race has forgotten somehow that the Unseen Realm is just as real as our physical world, for it's there that our desires begin to form. That is why, at this stage, you must get a clear mental picture of exactly what you want. For example, do you want a new apartment? Don't just wish for or picture any apartment in your mind. Be specific. Mentally see the neighborhood. Imagine the number of bedrooms. What about the rent? And so on. See yourself actually living there. Just be sure it's what you want, because you'll probably get it. You may speak your wish aloud also.

At this point I must address an issue I'm always asked about: Is it okay to visualize a lover? Sure! But remember...

Never, *never* visualize a real person. That is taboo in positive magical visualization. You may visualize the physical characteristics you like—tall, brunette, blue eyes, etc. But don't visualize that cute guy at work or the blonde across the street. You'll be asking for trouble.

By now you understand that at the conception stage of magical visualization, your desire and mental images must be clear. Let's move on.

Believe

For many, this is the hardest step in the visualization process, partly because you might not see anything happening in the physical world—that's normal. Once you've conceived your desire and have communicated it to the Unseen Realm through your mind's eye, it's time to let go. Now's the time to believe. Believe in your goal. Believe it will happen. Believe in yourself, and believe you darn well deserve it!

This is what happened to me. After a period of bad luck and sadness in my life, I tried some magical visualization to turn things around. Nothing happened. Later a psychic told me, "You feel that you deserve to suffer." She was *right*. After realizing I hadn't done anything to cause the situation, I began to truly believe in my visualization goal. Then things began to improve.

While you're in this "I believe" step, act like you've already achieved your wish. To help you understand what I mean, let's look again at the apartment visualization I mentioned in step 1. If that were my desire, now I'd act like I've found my new apartment. For example, I might go to a furniture store and look at a new sofa or TV for my "new" apartment. You don't need to actually buy anything. Just imagine that the visualization has come to fruition. This way you're telling the cosmos, "I believe this is going to happen."

My mantra is : Believe and you will receive.

Now, the last step...

Receive

To receive your vision naturally means your goal has physically manifested itself in your life. Now, in this final step of the process, it's time to give thanks to the Divine according to your spiritual path. This may include saying a simple prayer of thanks, lighting a candle, or leaving an offering on your altar.

If your wish is taking a long time to manifest, review what you've done. Was your vision clear? Did you speak Words of Power as part of the visualization? If so, did you clearly state what you wanted and did it match your vision? Or, like me, did you feel you didn't deserve it? See if you went off track and take the time to correct it.

If you received your wish and it wasn't exactly what you wanted, don't panic. You may redo the visualization, or be patient and let the Unseen Realm do its job. If, for instance, you go look at the apartment you think is going to be perfect and it isn't, just keep looking. Or if you think you've found your dream lover and they turn out to be a dud, you don't have to see the person again.

Keep in mind that you may receive something even better than what you visualized.

Magical Visualization Exercises

Here are a few exercises designed to help strengthen your ability to visualize. They will aid you by sharpening your focus and increasing your powers of imagination. Some require you to sketch, draw, paint, or color, but you don't need any artistic ability, so don't worry. Any art you create will be for your eyes only. The materials you'll need are inexpensive.

For the first exercise, you'll need one newspaper, some plain white paper, a pair of scissors, and a pencil. Look at the newspaper and find a photo that interests you. Cut it out, but leave the caption. Put the photo aside. Place a piece of plain white paper beneath the newspaper so it covers the hole where the photo was. Look at the photo one more time, then without looking at it, draw a rough sketch of the photo onto the white paper. You may read the caption to help you. Just sketch as much as you can recall. Do this as often as you wish.

This will get you warmed up for the next exercise.

．．．．．．．．．．．．・

For this exercise, you'll be able to focus on something you actually want. You'll need one miniature painting canvas or canvas board, acrylic or craft paint, a couple paint brushes, and a pencil.

First, I want you to ground and center. Then see in your mind's eye something you really want. See it coming to you, see yourself enjoying it. As you hold that vision in your mind, sketch it on the canvas. Now begin to apply the paint however you wish. Make it rich with detail. Is it a car you want? Paint it the color you want. Do you want a two-door or a four-door? Add that too. If it's a house you want, add shutters, flowers, a fence—whatever you want.

If you want, you may speak Words of Power affirming that this wish is coming to you. When finished, place your little painting on your altar where you can look at it, but don't obsess over it. Your wish is already taking shape in the non-physical world.

．．．．．．．．．．．．・

Sometimes you may need to visualize a human form. This visualization will help with that. All you'll need is a personal item from someone you know; they may be living or deceased. Any item will work—a scarf, a sweater, keys, or even a favorite mug.

Hold the item and close your eyes. Touch the item, and move your hands over it. See this person using or wearing the item. Hold this vision and open your eyes. Begin to add more details. If it's a key, see the person unlocking a door with it. If it's an article of clothing, see the person wearing it on a specific occasion. Complete the picture by hearing the person speak. Now, slowly let go of the vision and return to your everyday reality.

Soon you'll be able to visualize a person, real or imagined, quickly.

. . . .

Helping children with visualization helps increase their imagination. It also aids them in developing their comprehension skills, which helps them at school. This exercise is meant for kids, but adults can do it too. You'll need a fun children's book, white paper, pencils, and colored pencils or crayons.

Read the book to the child, but don't show them any of the pictures. When finished, give the child a piece of paper and a regular pencil. Tell them to sketch their favorite part of the story. They may ask to look at pictures in the book for an idea. I gently explain that I'd like to see the picture they have in their mind instead. I always tell them that there's no right or wrong way to do this.

Once they've completed their sketch, let them color it any way they want—it's okay if they have a purple cow! Then have them share the sketch with you and explain why it's their favorite part of the book.

I've done this many times and kids love it.

. . . .

Your ability to perform magical visualization will become easier the more you practice it. Your visualizations will become stronger, which in turn will make your magic more effective.

For the Witch or any other magical person, magical visualization helps us lead more powerful lives. With it you can create the reality you desire, and change your destiny.

James Kambos *is a writer and artist who enjoys studying folk magic and herbs. He lives in southern Ohio.*

Illustrator: Jennifer Hewitson

Miniature Megaliths: Create Your Own Stone Circles

Charlie Rainbow Wolf

Stonehenge. The very word conjures up a sense of ancient mysteries. Scientists and pilgrims alike have been searching to unlock its secrets. What is it that makes Stonehenge so fascinating? Megalithic circles are not uncommon in the British Isles; Stonehenge is probably just the most renowned. Although its name sounds ethereal, it really is only descriptive. A henge is a word used to describe a sizeable prehistoric earthwork. We mostly think of henges as being stone, but wood henges are also known. Therefore, the name Stonehenge merely describes what this megalith is: a henge made of stone.

Usually when we think of a stone henge, we think of ancient peoples. We might have ideas of Arthur, or the Druids, or perhaps we wonder at the physical challenges of raising the large and heavy stones. Where did they come from, and who put them there? I'll admit that most of the stone henges I have visited—includ-
ing Stonehenge, Castlerigg, and the stone circles that surround the village of Avebury—have been ancient. However, people today are still fascinated by the structures, and modern megaliths are even now being erected. Ivan McBeth has built several stone circles in the United Kingdom, while in the United States, Rob Roy runs Earthwood Building School in West Chazy, New York.

If you are like me, you probably don't have the room to erect a great stone monument—or the stamina to do so! However, if you find the energy of stones fascinating and you like working in a sacred space, then you can create your own miniature megalith, and it will be just as special and as useful to you as the great henges of old were to their creators.

Once you've become used to working with the stones, you will find it easy to put up a circle for a variety of uses and in many different places. I often carry a small black velvet pouch with a selection of tiny quartz crystals in it, just for this purpose. Those who are used to casting circles and working in sacred space will readily adapt to this; those new to the practice may take a bit longer. Either way, it is not complicated, nor expensive, to create your own stone circles.

Selecting Your Stones

The purpose of the circle might influence the choice of stone used. Here are some ideas.

QUARTZ

One reason I prefer using little quartz points is because quartz is a magnifier, and it will enhance whatever energy is cast upon it. Quartz, which is a form of silicon dioxide, contains every spectrum of light, and because of this, I find it to be the most versatile crystal to use. Variations on quartz include smoky quartz, amethyst, citrine, and rose quartz. They will all give a slightly different slant to the energy.

SMOKY QUARTZ

Smoky quartz is rather translucent and usually a shade of gray or brown. This form of quartz is very useful for grounding and removing negativity. In a miniature megalith, it could be employed for the purpose of lifting the mood, calming the nerves, and restoring balanced energy. Smoky quartz is also useful for magic to assist in manifesting wishes, and in prosperity magic.

AMETHYST

Amethyst is a very spiritual form of quartz, and resonates at a high frequency. It is no accident that the Pope's ring is amethyst. Amethyst points can be found in all shades of purple, from the lightest lilac to the darkest violet, and from nearly translucent to almost opaque. This stone is useful when seeking spiritual guidance, for magical pathworkings, and for enhancing intuition and incubating dreams. Amethyst also helps to bring emotional strength and stability.

CITRINE

Citrine stones are amethysts that have been exposed to great temperatures. Most of the commercially available citrines have been purposefully created rather than found in their natural state. Citrines have a similar opacity to amethysts, and range in color from a pale creamy white to a deep amber. Like amethysts, these stones can also be milky or fairly clear. Citrines, with their bright yellow hues, are happy stones, and make good company when building circles where creating joviality and cultivating optimism are the desired outcomes.

These descriptions should give you a few ideas, but the stones you select should be a matter of personal choice. There is absolutely no reason why you cannot use other crystals, or beach pebbles, or even driveway gravel. You might also consider using a combination of stones, with each different stone representing a different position in the circle being created.

Constructing the Stone Circle

Another aspect of working with miniature megaliths is the actual construction of the stone circle itself. There is no right or wrong way to do this, just as there is no right or wrong stone with which to work. It is the intent that is important.

One method of placing the stones is to base them on the interpretations of the astrological houses. Place twelve stones in a circle, to represent the wheel of the zodiac. Each stone can represent a different Sun sign, or it can represent a different energy or area of life. Those familiar with astrology or working with birth charts might find this a very easy type of stone circle to use.

Another method of placing the stones is to use one for each sabbat. This again would be a circle representing the seasons, timing, energies, and deities associated with each position. Both this and the astrological wheel are layouts that seem to be popular among people who use miniature megaliths. The circles can have a definite beginning and end, starting at the most appropriate position for the work being done.

In the medicine wheel used by some Native Americans, different stones, each representing a specific totem or spirit guardian, are used. For those who work with totems, this may be an appealing way to use a miniature megalith. It is possible to purchase stones that have the totems already carved into them, or, for a more personal touch, they can be painted. Sun Bear published an excellent book on working with the different energies of the medicine wheel, called *Dancing with the Wheel*.

A friend of mine has a bag of amethyst rune stones that she uses as her miniature megalith. Sometimes she casts a stone circle with all of

the runes, and sometimes she chooses specific runes with which to work. This way, not only is she doing the magical work, but she is also surrounded by the energies that specifically enhance the work being done. She finds this to be a very effective, portable, and versatile way of working with her own personal sacred space.

The runic emblems are just one type of figure that can be used on the stones in a miniature megalith. The glyphs for the planets, the signs of the zodiac, hieroglyphs, ogham, or other markings can also be used. It is possible that more than one set of stones might be desired, depending on what type of work is being done. I have to admit that I rather adhere to the belief that the less complicated things are, the better I can work with them. This is another reason why my miniature megalith is just a simple set of thirteen different quartz points, one for each month of a lunar year. Find what works for you, and stick with it.

Size should also be considered when working with the stones. If you have the space and the devotion, you could make a stone circle in your yard or garden in which to work. That would incline it to be a permanent structure. The charm of using tiny stones is that they are so portable. Pebbles, small crystals, or gemstone chips can be popped into a handbag or backpack, ever ready to offer their assistance when needed.

Working Magick in a Stone Circle

I have done ceremonies both inside a miniature stone circle and with a small group of people who surrounded the stone layout and used it as a focal point. Both methods were equally effective. Much depends on the number of people using the stones, the space available, and the purpose for which the circle is being raised.

Working inside the circle somehow seems to connect participants, regardless of the restrictions of time and space. There is something special about knowing that you are in the middle of a stone circle, gathering in a way that may have brought people together in the past, and in a way that continues to bring them together. People meet for ritual and celebration at stone monuments—old and new—throughout the world. Using the stones to cast the circle seems to set both intent and boundaries. By placing the stones in a particular pattern, sacred space can be created.

One way to lay the stones is for one person (perhaps the leader of the ritual) to put them, one at a time, around the people who are gathered for the magical working. In placing the last stone where he or she is going to stand, the leader casts a magic circle of protection. Invocations can be said as the stones are being placed, or reverent silence can be kept as everyone focuses their intent on what is about to happen.

If space is at a minimum, the stone circle can be placed on a table-top or other flat surface. In this way, it becomes a focal point for the work that is being done. Using this method, the ring of protection should be cast first, and then the stone circle created. Don't think that in using a smaller layout, the powers of the miniature megalith are depleted—they are not. Remember, the power lies with the people who are working the magic and what they are capable of producing. The stones are only there to assist.

Using a Portable Stone Circle

There are many ways of using a portable stone circle. In addition to being used for protection or as a focal point in ritual, the stones can be employed to put a ring of protection around someone or something until further assistance can arrive, perhaps in the case of a person or an animal who is not feeling well. Stone circles can also be erected to draw down the energies of particular planetary alignments, or mark specific sunrises and moonrises. A bit of astronomy and geometry might be needed for these, but it's not complicated. A good almanac or a basic ephemeris should be able to provide the information needed. Because the stones are pocket-sized, it's very easy to make adjustments should the calculations be a bit inaccurate. This can't be said of their larger counterparts!

. . . .

Using miniature megaliths can open up a whole new world of magic. It's not just about the stones, and about the circles; it's what they mean to you. From their origination centuries ago, these stone monuments have fascinated humankind. When working with our own stone circles, we link to that sense of wonder and also to the energies of the people who have been a part of stone circles throughout time. We pulse to the vibration of the actual stones, the bones of the earth. We reverberate with the energies of any glyphs we have put on the stones. More than that, though, we resonate with a part of ourselves—a part that is filled with the joy of exploration and the wonder of what we can find through connecting our own life force with that of All That Is.

SOURCES

Bear, Sun, Wabun Wind, and Crysalis Mulligan. *Dancing with the Wheel: The Medicine Wheel Workbook*. London: Simon & Schuster, 1991.

Roy, Rob. *Stone Circles: A Modern Builders Guide to the Megalithic Revival*. White River Junction, VT: Chelsea Green, 1999.

Charlie Rainbow Wolf *is happiest when she is creating something, especially if it can be made from items that others have cast aside. Pottery, writing, knitting, and Tarot are her deepest interests, but she happily confesses that she's easily distracted, because life offers so many wonderful things to explore. Charlie is the Dean of Faculty at the Grey School, where she teaches subjects in most of the sixteen departments. She is an advocate of organic gardening and cooking, and lives in the Midwest with her husband and special-needs Great Danes. www.charlierainbow.com.*

Illustrator: Kathleen Edwards

Awesome Altars on a Budget

Laurel Reufner

I still remember putting together my very first altar, just over two decades ago. Armed with information from Laurie Cabot's *Power of the Witch*, I diligently planned out what I would need. And then I tried to figure out where in the world I'd find it all in my small college town. Remember, we're talking the early '90s here. The biggest stores in town were Odd Lots, Ames, and Kmart.

Making the task even more daunting was my non-existent budget. I wasn't exactly a starving college student, since the kitchen held more than just ramen and toast, but there still wasn't much cash to spare. So, armed with a mental list, I set off for the local Odd Lots, where I hoped that the most stuff could be had for the least money.

Altar creation should be a joyful, thoughtful process. Here are some tips and suggestions to help you out with your own altar endeavors.

Before setting out to shop, you'll need to do a little homework. Go back through your books and notes, and make a list of what's suggested for your ritual altar. Now, ask yourself if you really think you will need or use everything on the list. Note which items you aren't sure about, and star or highlight the items you most want to find.

Where to Shop

Starting with the most-wanted items first, it's time to begin your search. Even small towns have some form of dollar store nowadays. Dollar General and Family Dollar are good places to look. And if you're lucky enough to have a Dollar Tree or Everything 99¢, then your budget is really going to love you. Grocery stores are another good place to scout out useful and affordable buys.

The main grocery store near my hometown has a small arts and crafts section—good for finding yarn and embroidery floss—as well as some housewares and a small automotive collection. Even if your store isn't that well stocked, most stores carry a small selection of kitchen tools, like measuring cups and such. You might be able to find something useful there.

If you don't mind having to perform a very thorough cleanse of your new tools, then try checking secondhand and antique shops. I'm lucky enough to work in an antique store close to where I now live, and I'm constantly amazed at the selection of goods on hand. I was thinking that I could put together a small altar just from stuff in the shop, except for an incense or oil burner, when lo and behold, I found a package of stick incense and a burner among some of the store owner's recent purchases. The only thing that I couldn't find is herbs. While you're shopping around, don't forget the yard sales and rummage sales. It's amazing what you can find once you start looking at things creatively.

Altar Tools

Most sources suggest building your stash of tools over time, waiting until the right tool for you comes along. However, how many of us really want to wait weeks, months, or even longer before we feel like we can fully start practicing? My suggestion is to buy inexpensive things now that will work for you and then replace them with items that feel even more perfect as time passes.

You can put together a basic, bare-bones altar for around twenty-five dollars if you shop wisely. You'll have even more leeway if you can allot fifty dollars for your purchases. What I'm going to try to do now is give you some suggestions for tools that will help you keep the cost down and yet still give you a lovely altar that you'll want to practice at. In the following paragraphs, I'm going to talk about the tools in the order in which I tend to place them on my altar.

Altar Cloth

I begin by defining my altar space. When we first moved to our new house, I had the luxury of using a 31 × 21-inch tabletop for an altar. (It was actually the old play table used by my sister and me, so it had added meaning.) Even with the entirety of the table to use for sacred space, I still put down some sort of cloth on it. Right now my altar is the top of a small bookshelf that used to be my mother's, and I've got a smaller piece of cloth on it. Using something to define the space just adds an extra layer to the energies going into the altar creation.

An altar cloth is also one of the easier "tools" to gather, since you may already have something around the house that can be repurposed. I've used remnants of fabric and fat quarters. Bandanas can now be found in a variety of patterns and colors and bought for as little as a dollar apiece, making it easy to pick up more than one to use on altars, letting you make them more seasonal. Decorative scarves are also useful, although they do tend to run a little more cost-wise.

Perhaps you want something other than cloth to define your space. How about a large decorative tray? Or maybe a big picture frame? Either could be made even more magical by decorating them for your ritual use. The tray can be painted or decoupaged with appropriate decorative papers and images. If you choose to use a picture frame, try to find a sturdy one at a secondhand shop, where it won't be as expensive as buying new. To personalize it, create a large enough image or collage to slip under the glass. If you have access to a computer, collages can easily be created with basic image manipulation software (GIMP is available for free) or electronic scrapbooking software. And images abound online.

Bamboo (or cloth) placemats would also work for a small altar. You might even be able to get your hands on a slab of wood that would be beautiful. I'm thinking of a round from a large tree, but even a length of board could work.

Candles

Next I set out my altar/illumination candles. Candles can serve many functions in Paganism, from providing illumination and helping set and define sacred space to standing in as representatives for divinities. Fortunately, it's a lot easier today to find a wide variety of colors—my first black candles were "over the hill" birthday candles. Even nicer is that glass-enclosed seven-day candles can now readily be found at grocery and dollar stores.

For illumination candles, I like to use either the seven-day jar candles or tapers set in pretty holders. I also have a small pair of Avon's Cape Cod goblets containing candles that I've used. They don't give off much light, but they belonged to my late father, so it's more of a nostalgia thing. As for pretty candle holders, they can be picked up at any dollar store for only a few dollars. This also would be a good item to scout out in secondhand stores or at yard sales.

Another way to use candles on your altar is to make them stand-ins for other representations of divinity. Candles are a lot less expensive than statues or many other representational items, so they're good for

small budgets. For this, I prefer to use pillars or tapers, mainly because of their heft and lasting power. If you just want a candle to represent the Goddess and the God, then go with silver and gold, if you can find them. If not, try white or gray for the Goddess and yellow for the God. And remember, white always works as a general color for just about any purpose. If you just want a representation of divinity in general, or maybe you just wish to honor the Goddess, or the God, then perhaps use a central pillar candle instead of a pair.

I also sometimes like to set a candle in the center of my altar in place of a chalice or cauldron. A candle works well as a center point for meditation or other focal needs. Of course, this might be my preference because I'm a fire sign in a house full of water and earth folks, but I know others who like to use a bowl or cauldron with water as their focal point.

Just as with trays, candles are very easy to customize. You can carefully carve appropriate symbols in them, dress them with various scents, or even wrap bands of decorative paper around them. Jar candles are particularly easy to embellish, because there's less worry about keeping your papers and other pretties from catching fire.

Finally, remember to pay attention to the scent of candles when buying them. The one thing that is hard to do nowadays is to find unscented candles. Usually the jar candles are scentless, as are white emergency candles and some votives and tealights. However, tapers, votives, and pillars all seem to be scented, at least in the places where we shop. If you're lucky enough to have an actual craft store in your town, then you might get lucky and find scentless candles.

Focal Point: Candle, Chalice, or Cauldron

Usually the next item on my altar is some sort of focal point. This could be a candle (as mentioned earlier), a chalice, or a bowl or cauldron. It all depends on what the ritual purpose is going to be, and that is something that only you can decide. Use what works or what you feel the most drawn to.

Let's start with the chalice as a focal piece. It's basically just a water goblet or stemmed glass or cup. Once you look at it that way, all kinds of possibilities open up. Find a pretty goblet at the store and you're good to go. If it's around mid- to late fall, you might even luck into finding a cauldron-shaped candle holder or candy dish in the Halloween decorations. Our local Dollar Tree has a beautiful selection of cheap goblets. Large seashells will also work well, especially if you are drawn to the element of water or want to create an all-natural altar setup. And if you want to create a mini or travel altar, a small seashell or even an acorn cap would work.

An inexpensive cauldron can be a bit trickier to find. Traditionally it's a small brass or cast-iron vessel that can hold fire or water, but those are usually beyond our suggested budgets. Since odds are that you're only going to use your cauldron as a vessel for water or perhaps to drop lit paper or herbs into, then a heatproof clay or glass bowl set on a heat-resistant tile would work just as well until you can swing the cost of something more traditional. It would also buy you time to search for a cauldron that you like.

REPRESENTATION OF DEITY

Next comes some representation of the deities. As mentioned earlier, candles are a great, inexpensive choice, but they aren't the only possibility. Small figurines that have spiritual meaning to you will also work, such as unicorns, angels, or dragons. Dollar stores in particular can be great places to find statuary that would look completely in place on your altar.

You can also find items in nature that work wonderfully, such as smooth, round stones for the feminine (especially if they have a hole or hollow in them) and more rectangular-shaped stones for the masculine. An acorn or a pine cone would also work for the God figure, as would an apple or pomegranate or perhaps a small pot of ivy or violets for the Goddess.

SALT AND WATER

I like to have small dishes of salt and water on my altar, which are easy enough to take care of inexpensively. Sea salt can often be found at a reasonable price, even at some dollar stores, such as Dollar Tree, but regular table salt works just as well. The water can come from the tap, from a bottle of spring or distilled water, or from rain or ocean water that you've collected. If you don't live near the ocean but know someone heading that way on vacation, ask them to bring some back for you. As for the dishes, any small container will do. I've used glass condiment cups and pretty ceramic dishes. Shells would also be nice. Heck, in a pinch, grab a couple of bottle caps. The salt could even be carefully piled atop a small, flat rock.

Incense

Next comes the incense. Keeping in mind that we're shopping on a small budget in a small town, we're going to be pretty much limited to sticks and cones, since finding charcoal tablets might be impossible. And whatever you do, don't use regular grilling charcoal! The briquets give off a vapor that is very dangerous to inhale, especially in an enclosed space.

Incense burners are pretty easy to find, especially the plain, long wooden ones. However, if you really want to save those pennies, a bowl filled with salt, sand, or even dirt can work as a holder. Heck, you could easily tuck a stick of incense down into a potted plant and be good to go. Just remember to remove and dispose of the remaining bits of sticks every so often.

Finding incense for your purposes might be a little trickier. You'll need to poke around in the grocery and dollar stores to see what you can find. You might even want to check at gas stations and convenience stores. Those places sometimes have little gift-like displays and selections of incense and burners. You might even find some altar statuary there as well.

If you are lucky enough to find incense charcoal but need a burner, try using a clay dish or flower pot filled with salt or sand as your burner. The salt will help absorb the heat from the burning charcoal.

If you don't want to deal with incense smoke, you might want to consider using a small oil burner and fragrance oils. Small burners can often be found inexpensively.

Athame

My first athame was a pretty letter opener, claimed from the man who is now my husband. Since the athame isn't necessarily supposed to be sharp, letter openers are great substitutes if you can't find an actual

affordable knife. (And truth be told, I eventually gave mine up, since it was one of those things I just never used.)

WAND

Wands are something else that I don't often use, but I still like to have one on the altar. And they are one of the easiest altar tools to obtain with little fuss or expense. Here are just a few ideas to get you thinking. Drawn to Bast? Use a cat toy. Tree branches work well, decorated with bits of wire, beads, and ribbon, or left plain. I've used a cinnamon stick and a vanilla bean in the past, as well as short, narrow pieces of driftwood. And in a pinch, your pointer finger will do the job.

PENTACLE

One of the final tools that I need to mention is the altar pentacle. I've never had an actual one, although I have used similar items. I'll often place a small plate or tray atop the altar to hold items of offering and such. Trays and plates suitable for the task can be found just about anywhere, and it's easy to build up a small selection, giving you options for the various seasons or other ritual needs.

If you definitely want an actual altar pentagram, try using a small circle of wood with the pentacle either burnt or painted on. Another way to create an altar pentacle involves taking a clear glass plate and decoupaging the bottom of it. If space is a consideration, try using a clear glass candle plate.

· · · · · · · · · · · ·

I think that just about covers the basic altar tools, except for perhaps the broom, and I'm sure you're thinking creatively enough now that you can figure that one out on your own. This same type of creative thinking can also help you stock your magical cabinet with supplies while still going easy on your wallet. Over time you'll be able to replace your original, basic, inexpensive tools with fancier and more expensive counterparts—if you decide that you want to. Just remember to keep your eyes open to the possibilities around you.

Laurel Reufner's *mother can verify that she grew up a "wild child" in farming country. Laurel has been earth-centered for around a quarter century and really enjoys writing about whatever topics grab her attention. She has always lived in southeastern Ohio and currently calls Athens County home, where she lives with her wonderful husband and two wild daughters of her own. Find her online at* Laurel Reufner's Lair, *http://laurelreufner .blogspot.com, or on Facebook.*

Illustrator: Christa Marquez

An Offering on Offerings

Blake Octavian Blair

This situation might be a familiar one: You're ready to invoke a spirit or deity to aid you in your magickal working. You know what you need help with or want to accomplish, you've checked your astrological timing, you have your ritual-working all laid out. But wait, have you thought about what you're going to give as an offering to the spirit whose aid you are invoking?

Choosing an Offering

There are many ways to determine what would make a good offering for a specific deity or spirit. Offerings are important to show your gratitude to the spirit for the assistance you are asking it to provide to you. There are several things to keep in mind when determining what you will offer. First, it's important to know that not all offerings will be appropriate for all deities. It's important to choose something that will be pleasing and not offensive to the entity you are petitioning for assistance. A good place to begin would be to research both the specific spirit and its culture of origin. You would not want, for example, to offer non-vegetarian food or liquor to the Hindu god Ganesha; however, the lwa of Vodou absolutely love liquor. On the other hand, Lord Ganesha undeniably loves candy and *ladoo* (an Indian sweet), among other sweets and fruits.

Another thing to consider is that a good offering often relates to the deity's goals and purpose. For example, Ogun of the African diasporic religions is known as a god of iron. An appropriate offering for him could consist of a handful of iron nails or an iron horseshoe. One aspect of the Egyptian goddess Bast is that she is seen as a protectress of felines. A possible offering to consider for her would be to grow and tend to a catnip plant, some of which could be offered to your pet cats! (That act in itself would be pleasing to Bast.) Cultural dishes from the spirit's native cuisine are almost always met with good reception as well. The Hindu god of love, Krishna, would be greatly pleased by a wonderfully rich dish of Indian curry.

In addition to choosing things that are favored by the individual spirit, things that are culturally relevant, or things that relate to the spirit's prowess, you can offer things that are of importance and value to you personally. Spirits are greatly pleased when you make the effort to honor them with practices and offerings that are elements of their native culture. However, I have found from personal experience that they will also respond favorably if you honor them in ways relevant to you in your own life and culture, providing they are not taboo to the specific spirit. Many will even view it as

an honor that you are sharing special things from your own world-view, while still acknowledging theirs, much as you would with an honored guest. It is my personal experience that spirits and deities are generally not bound by culture. If the item you want to offer has relevance to you, many spirits will recognize that and see that you respect them highly enough to sacrifice that particular item as a gift in their name. These offerings can come in many forms, including food, money, time, and service. Let's look a little closer at some of these options.

While food offerings were mentioned earlier, there are a few more things that could be said in regard to the personal relevance of the offering. A meal you have prepared with your own hands not only exemplifies your willingness to share your food (a gesture seen to be generally honorable cross-culturally) but also speaks of the time and energy you put into its creation. Store-bought items such as cookies,

 crackers, sweets, and the like are not unacceptable offerings, but it is always better to give something you have made yourself, whenever possible. Offering a plate of food that you cooked yourself has a lot more relevance and value than something prepackaged that you pulled out of your cupboard as an afterthought. You can even offer the deity a little bit of what you made for your family dinner if the food items are acceptable for the spirit. A plate of food from the family dinner makes an especially effective offering for ancestral spirits (such as with the practice of having a "dumb supper" at Samhain), making them feel included in household activities and the day-to-day life of the family.

Making a work of art or completing a craft project as an offering to a deity is also an excellent exchange of energy worth offering. Perhaps the deity you're working with is associated with a certain gemstone. You can create a devotional offering that you can use to carry the blessing of that deity with you everywhere you go. An example of accomplishing this is to create a necklace made of beads of the deity's associated gemstone, incorporating other corresponding symbolism, consecrating it in the name of that deity, and wearing it as a connective offering. Some deities, such as the goddess Brigid, have handicrafts that are specifically related to them. Brigid's cross is a simple craft that, when finished, makes a wonderful protection talisman to hang in your home. If you have an artistic talent, do not hesitate to put it into action to paint, sew, sculpt, or draw a unique offering.

One old standby offering that anyone can use their artistic ability to personalize is that of the glass-encased novena candle, alternately referred to as a seven- or nine-day candle. Purchase one with plain glass and then decorate it with imagery specific to the spirit or deity you wish to offer it to. You can simply draw symbols on it with a magic marker, or print out a picture of the deity and glue it to the glass. You can even get as elaborate as decoupaging a whole collage, or hand-painting a masterpiece on the glass.

One of the simplest and oldest offerings is that of incense. Its use is mentioned in one of the world's oldest religious texts, the Hindu Vedas, dating back about 3,000 years. Incense is a part of the practice of many different religions, including Native American spirituality, Christianity, Hinduism, Buddhism, and Islam, among others. Different spirits are known to have their individual preferences of scent, in addition to scents that are favored by their culture as a whole. Incense is another item you can craft yourself using various dried herbs and resins. Oftentimes, very effective rituals can consist of the simple offering of just a bit of incense and a heartfelt prayer.

This brings us to another poignant offering: that of your words. Whether they be spoken, written, chanted, or sung, your words can serve as a powerful offering even when you have nothing else. With all the time, energy, and creative effort put into the composing of a prayer, song, poem, or chant, it holds an enormous amount of heartfelt magickal energy. There are many wonderful books on this topic that you can reference for further ideas and assistance with this type of offering. We all have our words to offer in the absence of all else, whether we simply write them on a piece of parchment as a petition or outwardly express them in song.

Another form of offering that people often overlook is that of performing community service. Perhaps you are asking the goddess Laxmi to aid in bringing you prosperity. A fitting offering would be donating your time to helping those less prosperous, such as by helping serve meals at a local soup kitchen. This would also be befitting when honoring goddesses of the hearth and home, such as Brigid or Hestia. Taking time to clean up trash from public places such as city parks or roadway medians would be an appropriate way to donate time to nature spirits and deities. As we have discussed, your time is valuable, so why not donate your time to a cause that is valuable to the spirit you're working with? If you're working with an ancestral spirit, you could assist an organization that supports a cause the ancestor was passionate about. If they were an animal lover, you could donate time helping at your local Humane Society!

Making Your Intention Clear

Of course, once your offerings are chosen, a whole host of other questions and issues arise. First, it's important to make your intentions for the terms of the offering clear to the deity or spirit you're working with. Is this offering a complete gift, or do you wish to take it back after you've offered it in order to carry the attributes and blessings of the deity with you? Whatever your intention, be sure to let the deity know at the time of offering. If you plan to ask a spirit for assistance with the promise of an offering of thanks, or in payment after you have received their assistance, be sure to lay out exactly in what form that offering will be made, what it's for, and when it will be given.

Some spirits have quite strong and swift personalities, and any confusion might have an unpleasant result!

What to Do with Your Offerings

The question eventually arises of what to do with these offerings after you have given them. Of course, you can let them remain in the shrine or on the altar of the deity. Some of the most beautiful and energetically powerful shrines have copious collections of offerings in them representing the longstanding and powerful relationship between the deity and the devotee. However, some offerings such as food and fresh flowers cannot be left indefinitely on an altar. A proper way to handle these would be to consume any edible offerings before they become inedible—if it is permissible by the spirit or deity. This is, in fact, the custom in many religions, including Hinduism,

Buddhism, and many indigenous Pagan traditions. In Hinduism, the offered and blessed food is called *prasad* and is very auspicious to consume.

Should a food offering become inedible, the best way to handle this is likely to leave it in nature to decompose or assist in feeding wildlife. When it comes to the offering of fresh-cut flowers, it is considered by many cultures extremely inauspicious to have wilting and desecrated flowers in the home and especially on an altar. Remove flowers as soon as they show obvious signs of being past their prime. However, do not overlook the possibility of offering potted flowers and then planting them in your garden or in a pot on your patio. Purchasing a houseplant to offer to a deity and then placing it in the home is also a wonderful way to honor and energetically foster a *growing* relationship with the spirit.

Sometimes offered items will find their own individual way of "moving on." We are all familiar with the phenomenon of finding an item we know is meant to be ours and that ends up coming home with us. Sometimes we possess items that we know need to go to a new home with others. You may have the intuition strike you that a person you know needs a blessing or energetic boost in the area that a deity presides over. For example, perhaps you offered the goddess Brigid a handmade Brigid's cross, and you have a friend who is attempting to recover from surgery. You may have the intuition that your friend needs the blessing of healing energy and that you'd like to gift them with the cross. Simply communicate in your own way with Brigid to see if this transaction is okay with her. If permission is granted, pass the blessed item along to the person who needs it.

You'll find over time that deities will be energetically willing to part with some items, yet they will resoundingly respond that they wish not to have other items removed! Use your natural gift of intuition when communing with deities and spirits of any sort.

Whatever their decision, I find that in many cases it is in our best interest not to question their desire.

. . . .

Offerings are an important part of your relationship with divine entities. They provide a means of worship, payment, and energetic exchange vital to magickal work. It's likely that the best way to choose the method of finding the appropriate offering will become apparent to you as you plan your specific working. After all, for everything the divine offers us, the least we can do is offer something of ourselves in return.

Suggested Reading/Bibliography

Barrette, Elizabeth. *Composing Magic: How to Create Magical Spells, Rituals, Blessings, Chants, and Prayers.* Franklin Lakes, NJ: New Page Books, 2007.

Illes, Judika. *Encyclopedia of Spirits: The Ultimate Guide to the Magic of Fairies, Genies, Demons, Ghosts, Gods & Goddesses.* New York: HarperOne, 2009.

Oxtoby, Willard G. *World Religions: Eastern Traditions.* Second edition. Don Mills, Ontario: Oxford University Press, 2002.

Blake Octavian Blair *is an eclectic Pagan, ordained minister, shamanic practitioner, writer, Usui Reiki Master-Teacher, tarot reader, and musical artist. Blake blends various mystical traditions from both the East and West along with a reverence for the natural world into his own brand of modern Neo-Paganism and magick. Blake holds a degree in English and Religion from the University of Florida. He is an avid reader, crafter, and practicing vegetarian. Blake lives with his beloved husband, an aquarium full of fish, and an indoor jungle of houseplants. Visit him online at www.blakeoctavian blair.com or write him at blake@blakeoctavianblair.com.*

Illustrator: Tim Foley

Work the Magic!

Boudica Foster

While listening to conversations when I am at events or with a group of Pagans who are magic workers, I often hear, "I've been studying Witchcraft now for x amount of years." I usually ask, "So how many spellworkings have you done?" It is disheartening to hear the reply, "None yet."

Further discussion will usually bring up some fears or concerns, or maybe the person is just not ready. I then ask, why all the studying if you are not going to eventually delve into the magic? This becomes tricky. I never want to push someone into something if they are not ready, but when someone talks about

I never want to push someone into something if they are not ready, but when someone talks about "studying magic" for years, maybe they need to look at why they still haven't *worked* magic.

"studying magic" for years, maybe they need to look at why they still haven't *worked* magic.

There are many reasons for this. Some people just never make it past the study phase with magic. Fear is one of the more common reasons: fear of failure, fear of making a mess, or fear of doing it wrong. There are so many books that attach horrible warnings to working magic that it is very understandable that fear can be the big stumbling block when it comes to magic.

But let's examine some of the root causes of those fears. Let's look beyond those fears and work on some personal magic. It's time to make the magic happen!

One of the main concerns is, what happens if something is done wrong that really gets out of control? What happens if a spell unintentionally creates so much power that it threatens the entire fabric of time and space? Sounds dramatic, doesn't it? But some concerns are genuine. What if we do create a spell that is too powerful for us to handle? Or we just do it wrong?

With all the new people trying out their skills in the magical arts, if someone had really messed up big time, don't you think the earth would have flung off its axis already and we would have faced Armageddon by now? Don't you think that if someone really wanted to do something evil, it would have happened by now?

Some people will argue that we are already facing some of the most evil magic in this world today. I beg to differ. Much of the evil in this world does not come from magic, but is caused by humans being careless with the environment, or is just a byproduct of human greed, envy, and hatred. Sorry, no magic involved. We have managed to mess up our lives and our world without a hint of magic. We are personally responsible for our condition in life.

But we do see magic every day. The fact that we are still here in spite of all the humanmade chaos suggests that there is enough magical energy in this world to hold us together for a good long time. I believe we have spun just enough magical energy to enable

us to work toward solutions we can use to confront the mess we have and clean it up to make a better world for all of us. I do not believe that the gods get total credit for the fact that we have made it through this last century, no more than they get credit for the mess we have before us. I believe humankind and magic have also enabled us to survive through some of the most trying times humanity has ever encountered. The fact that Paganism and the Craft have made such a resurgence in our time speaks of their importance. There are universal checks and balances. I believe we are the balance. We are responsible for what we do, and continue to do. Yes, we can make a further mess of things if we are not careful. But we hold the solutions, and magic can make them apparent.

In his book *Magick in Theory and Practice*, Aleister Crowley managed to explain magic. To paraphrase and condense his work, he states that magic is the means by which we bring about change through our will. He then goes on with some pretty deep writing on how to do this. Well, he was writing a book. I believe it is much simpler than all that, and I don't need volumes to explain the basics.

The Basic Elements of Spellwork

So let's start with the basic elements of spellwork. I would like to break it into a few moving parts: intent, energy, and change. Intent is composed of desire and plan by our will. Energy is the method we use to achieve our desire and work the plan. And change is the final outcome of our spellwork.

Intent is personal aspiration. It is the purpose of our working. This needs to be extremely clear when we are working magic in order for us to achieve success. We need to plan out exactly how we are going to achieve our goal. Intent and plan are the first elements to working magic. What do we want, and how will we go about getting it? We very carefully define what we want and plot out a course of action.

We then seek out the most likely elements to help us get to our goal. We put together a course of action to follow, a plan. Magic works hand in hand with the mundane actions we do every day. Without mundane actions, magic will just sit there and stare back at us, waiting for a plan to be implemented.

In all things, if we do not have a plan for what we want, we cannot expect to achieve our goal. That has always been the downfall of miracles. You have heard the phrase "waiting for a miracle to happen." Yes, the gods may gift us with something awesome on occasion. But it is the nature of the gods to give it to us when they are ready, if ever at all. I believe the gods, or the universe, have already given us the means. All we need to do is exercise those means.

If we look at many things that are cataloged as "miracles," we will find that many of them are attributable to some form of mundane accompaniment. We think, oh, it's a miracle that someone lived after such an accident or illness. But upon closer examination, we find that the person had a lifesaving operation performed by a skilled doctor and was cared for by experienced staff at a hospital. Or they received a new treatment for their illness that was created by an expert research staff. While the gods may have inspired the research staff, or given some special set of skills to the doctors or hospital staff, it was the work of the individuals who assisted in performing that "miracle" that really made it happen. Or we think that it was a miracle that a particular person won the lottery. Actually it was that person purchasing a lottery ticket with the right numbers that made it happen. Maybe the universe inspired that person with the right numbers, but if that person had not purchased a ticket, then it wouldn't have happened. Mundane actions combined with energy and a plan created change in that person's life.

Intent is motivated by our will. We will something to be. Will is the plan; it is the first essential step in making magic work. So pick up a pencil and write down what you want—set a goal. Then figure out how to achieve it. What skills, prep work, and essential elements do you need? Wishing is not going to make it happen. And if you wait for that "miracle" to happen, you may be waiting all your life.

This is quite easy to do, and should take just a couple of days to work into an exact plan with your goals clearly set out before you. Pick up that pencil right now, get a sheet of paper, and start working your magic.

Intent and planning are not the total sum of magic. With intent there must be change. We want to do something; we are changing what is already in place. What is needed to make this change is energy. Magical energy implements the plan that we designed. It is a simple formula: intent, a plan to achieve our goals, and then the energy necessary to make the changes happen by our will. Magic is very simple, really, once it's broken down into its working parts.

In my universe, we all draw this energy from the same source. What makes it different is the path this energy takes to get to us. Whether through crystals, plant material, elements, or the energy of the universe, it is energy for us to use to achieve our intent. The way the energy comes to you will be determined by what you want to achieve, how you want to achieve it, and when you want to have it happen. Do not mistake energy for the gods. Even the gods draw from that energy pool. They just have a much better method of doing so. We are still learning; they have perfected it.

Energy is not picking up a crystal or a wand and zapping something into existence. Rather, energy is what you put into a working to make things change. You have your intent clearly stated, and you have a plan worked out as to how you want to achieve that goal. Guess what? Now you just have to put some energy into working your magic. Continue on with your plan till you achieve your goal, and you have worked your first magic spell!

Wait, you are not seeing the magic? What exactly are you looking for? Are you expecting something to happen just because you want it to? Well, because we are mortal beings, the only way things are going to happen is if we make them happen. We do not create; we change. The first thing magic changes is us. The change is in how we achieve success. Ideas and goals that seem beyond our reach aren't anymore. When we achieve these goals with some measure of success, it means we have created change in our lives beyond what we expect from ourselves. This is the magic. Magic is not a silver bullet to cure everything; it is a vehicle to get us to the point where we change to make our hopes and aspirations a reality.

It seems that people will try multiple ways of achieving a magical working rather than focusing on one method till it works. What we need to do is focus on one method first and achieve success with that, and then we can move on to something a bit more advanced. Yes, we need to take baby steps before we can run. We seem to want instant gratification, but magic does not work that way. You may have to do a spellworking several times with many steps before you achieve success.

Examine your intent and see if you were clear in what you hoped to achieve. Is your goal clearly stated? Is it attainable? Play with the plan; see if you left out something essential needed to make the plan work. Or maybe you don't have the right tools. Does your plan contain enough of the necessary elements and skills you need to accomplish your intent? Examine your energy. Have you invested enough energy to make it successful? Or have you overshot your mark and poured all sorts of energy into a project that will never get off the ground?

Remember, there are universal checks and balances in all things. Whether you want to call it divine intervention or the universal consciousness, there are certain goals that we cannot or will not be allowed to achieve. Take a look at your intent and ask yourself, is this really something I should expect? Maybe the universe is telling you otherwise. Always be careful what you work toward; sometimes it will be something you did not expect or want.

In magic, we work to achieve—and we get results. There are people still waiting for a miracle to happen. Pick up the wand and make your magic happen. Start small and start now. There is no time like the present to start achieving your intent.

Boudica Foster *is best known for her professional reviews of books on Paganism and its various paths. Boudica and her husband ran the successful Wiccan/Pagan Times website till they retired it recently to pursue other ventures. She also ran the Zodiac Bistro website, a repository of articles, commentaries, and reviews by Boudica, for many years till she retired that recently as well. She is a self-published author.*

Boudica is a staunch supporter of building Pagan community and has worked in covens as well as having a solitary practice. In the past she has presented at many events in the Northeast and Ohio. She still presents occasionally at events and holds public workshops in the Northeast. She runs an online bookstore and reads tarot cards for clients. Boudica lives in Bucks County, Pennsylvania, with her husband of many years and her cats.

Illustrator: Rik Olson

Building a Child's Book of Shadows

Natalie Zaman

One November afternoon longer ago than I'd like to admit, I was strolling down Essex Street in Salem, Massachusetts, with my daughter, enjoying the post-Halloween emptiness. Running ahead, she paused in front of a shop window and then beckoned to me to catch up. When I did, I found her admiring the display: a single, magnificent, leather-bound book.

It was a Book of Shadows. No, it was the *ultimate* Book of Shadows: two hundred sheets of gilt-edged paper, handbound in a volume that looked as if it had been sitting on one of Merlin's library shelves for the last thousand years. The book was blank save for the first page, where a spell had been elaborately inked. "A real spell by a real Witch," the enthusiastic shopkeeper told me. It was, of course, expensive—but I confess, even with the real spell by a real Witch, I *wanted* it. My daughter wanted one, too.

"It's the most beautiful book in the world," she said.

I guessed that she was comparing it to the only other magical journal she knew: mine. Even then, in its umpteenth volume, it was written in different inks from when my pen ran out, and was filled with cross-outs, and bits and pieces stapled in. Still, time and experience had given my humble book its own beauty—and with this thought, the beginnings of a lesson emerged.

"That's something to save up for," I said, and thanking the real Witch, we left the store and headed for Staples.

Practical Magic

The book in the Salem shop definitely has its place (a gift for a rite of passage comes to mind), but it would be an extravagant starter journal for an eleven-year-old. My original intention was to purchase a plain blank book for my daughter and then explain how she should be inspired by what she'd seen to decorate and fill it herself. But as we picked through the array of faux leather and printed covers, I realized that she would need some guidance.

Our family's practices are informal. Making a Book of Shadows—and experiencing the inevitable tweaks, trials, and mistakes that are a part of the process—would bring some order to my children's magical training. The English teacher in me begged that I start this project with some proven study habits: discipline and organization.

Ditching the blank books, we headed for the school supplies. The Book of Shadows we would create would be more high school than Hogwarts, but hopefully we would turn a collection of mundane objects into something special—true alchemy.

Shopping List for a Child's Book of Shadows

- **A ringed binder.** It might not have the old-world charm of a leather-bound book, but it's far more practical in that pages are easy to add and rearrange.

- **Paper.** Keeping the pages in a binder allows for the incorporation of colors and textures—including the occasional slice of handmade parchment.

- **Plastic sleeves.** These provide not only protection, but also a means to store small objects related to the work you're doing (stones, cards, feathers, etc.). We keep things organized by using different-colored sleeves, and when only clear ones are available, we line the outside edges with patterned or colored masking tape (also good for repairs!).

- **Pens, pencils, markers, crayons, stickers, and other writing and art supplies.** Eventually we incorporated photocopies, computer print-outs, and writings and artwork by other people. (It is a marvelous thing to have a beloved relative or friend write or draw in your Book of Shadows.) However, putting pen to paper connects person to idea, whether you're writing in your own book or you're making notes on someone else's work. This is also an effective method for remembering information.

Dividing and Conquering

We had the raw materials. The next question was, where to begin? I let my children's interests be our guide. Just as in their school notebooks, we made dividers for each subject. As we worked, some subjects were shelved for lack of interest, time, or resources. Interestingly, the ones that stuck also had a practical bent, an aspect of the spiritual that could somehow be connected to a necessary awareness in day-to-day life. While each child's approach to these topics has changed over time, we began with a set structure. Our "Binder of Shadows" continues to do its work; it has set a foundation of good habits that, even when left for a time, can easily be picked up again.

DREAMWORK

Dreams were an easy subject to start with, because everyone experiences them. I'd learned that interpreting the meaning of a dream is more complex than simply looking up remembered imagery for its symbolic value. My dream experience was richer when I approached interpretation in a methodical manner: be observant and be detached.

I've tried to teach my children that there are very few instances in life where one needs to react to make a decision. Why not hit that principle home in the spiritual quarter, too? When my daughter has a dream, I encourage her to record it in the section of her Book of Shadows devoted exclusively to dreamwork using this method, which is explored in great detail in The Jungian-Senoi Dreamwork Manual by Strephon Kaplan-Williams:

Write down the dream verbatim as if you're writing out the details of a movie you've seen. There's only so much time the human brain has to recall the details of REM activity, so be in the habit of keeping paper and pencils next to your bed so you can record everything as soon as possible after waking. After the "facts" are down—written or drawn—then record any emotional and physical reactions.

Put a bit of time-distance between yourself and the dream before interpreting it. Use dream and symbol dictionaries to discover traditional and alternative meanings behind objects, colors, animals, etc., but also try to connect the dream to situations in your waking life. Explore all possibilities. Here is where keeping a Book of Shadows in a binder comes in handy; look for connections made to material in *other* sections of your book. Could the dream have something to do with spellwork that you've done? Your astrology? If so, make copies or write notes to cross-reference so that the information can be kept together.

Keeping interpretation, reaction, and straight recording prioritized and separate makes for keener observation (a good life skill), and the dreams themselves take on a new significance. I've seen frightening night visions become less so after they've been broken down. Examining prophetic dreams grounds them and strengthens intuition.

When it comes to dreams, time is relative. **Track and trace synchronicities, patterns, and repetition** and keep that information organized. You may discover connections days, weeks, months, or even years later.

Sabbats

Figuring out why we do what we do has been a bit of an obsession of mine, and one I've passed on to my youngest son. One of the things we love about exploring the past is the touchstone it provides to the now. Ancient traditions are fascinating, but when you can relate them directly to your own life, a deeper appreciation and understanding emerges.

I tried to get my son to connect the spirit of the seasons to things going on in his life. Many times this would start as a conversation that would sometimes lead to a field trip, project, or writing prompt (I had to use the latter sparingly; kids can smell a homework assignment from a mile away). For example, here is a prompt we did at Yule where we talked about fear of the dark:

> People have always feared the darkness. When it is difficult to see, and your other senses (including your super-senses) take over, the spirit world feels strong and so close that you can almost touch it. This can be uncomfortable. No wonder people did rituals at the winter solstice (the longest night of the year) to make sure the sun's strength would return! What are you afraid of, and why? Shine light on your fears by brainstorming strategies for overcoming them.

This prompt tied my son's fears—the darkness and the unknown—to the time of year (Yule) and the impending change that comes with the changing season (Imbolc). As with any issue, it took time and trial and error to resolve. We kept a copy of this journal entry with the eventual meditation we concocted (in the section for spellwork), and saw it as a positive step toward overcoming the fear.

We've discovered that cross-referencing (and the resulting ability to recollect information quickly, not to mention the self-assurance that comes when you're sure of what you're saying and doing) doesn't always come as second nature to everyone. Exercises like this one help to develop and hone skills like these that are useful not only in magic, but in everyday life.

SPELLWORK

Magic is a power that comes from within and must be used wisely. I've tried to teach my children that casting a spell is a multistep process that can and should be documented. Admittedly, the process is slow, but worth the time—especially when it works.

Write out what you want or are trying to accomplish. The simple act of writing something out makes it more real. One starts

with an intention, a "thing" that can be neither touched nor seen. But when an intention is written down, it is given a physical form. Next—and just as important—**write down WHY you want this, and keep asking "Why?" as much as you can.** This act encourages the spellcaster—adult or child—to think about their intentions and what's motivating them, and to dig to the heart of the matter: What is it you *really* want? My oldest son wanted to do some magical work to ensure success in a school subject he was struggling with, but in examining the why, he came to the conclusion that what he really wanted was to be confident in the material he was studying. He ended up doing a meditation for focus, discipline, and guidance— not a quick fix, but a lasting solution. (This eventually came in the form of a few dedicated teachers and a tutoring program.)

Once the goal is established, **make a touchstone—and record the steps of its creation.** Looking at a touchstone stimulates the mind (THE most important magical tool) to remember the purpose of the spell and send instant energy to it. Write out all the details: How did you come up with the idea? What materials did you use to make it, and why? Did you do your crafting at a specific time (season, moon phase, etc.)? What was your process? These steps provide an opportunity to practice creating a sacred space in which to work, and to expand knowledge about magical tools, timing, and other topics as they apply.

Add some action—and again, record what you did. Adding physical action to a spell keeps the energy around it alive. Action includes actual physical activity and speaking intentions aloud. Again, it's important to record what was done and what was said—including any feelings, premonitions, and sensations that occurred when the action was executed.

Finally, **keep track of your progress.** Was your work efficacious? Did you see signs of it right away, or did it take time to manifest? Or maybe the spell didn't work at all—it happens. Keeping a record of what was done helps in spotting mistakes, finding where improvements can be made, and making connections to other work. Write down any changes, dreams, and synchronicities that could be connected to your spell for as long as it takes— you might see effects years later. If you have corresponding sections in your Book of Shadows, make copies or notes and keep the information together in all sections to cross-reference and make

connections. Working magic is like dropping a stone in a pond: the ripples reverberate for a long time before the water stills again. Be aware of how your actions—and magic—affect other people, and other areas of your life.

Writing for Life

Since my children each started their own Book of Shadows, we've added sections on moon phases, divination, healing modalities, and personal reflection.

I wish I could say that this method is perfect. It isn't. Life gets in the way, and practices are neglected. Skills rust, facts and formulas are forgotten, and things get lost. Many times we've had to reorganize, review, fix mistakes, and even start over. As my children get older, privacy comes into question. Sometimes as a teacher, I've had to let go of control and allow change to happen. Structure has its place, but spirituality, like nature, is spontaneous and ever evolving—and meant to bring comfort and pleasure, not stress.

Like the authors, these Books of Shadows are always growing and changing. It is a marvelous thing to witness, and it all begins with a blank page.

RESOURCES

It's never too late or too early to begin building a Book of Shadows with your child. There are a growing number of resources for Pagan families, both in print and online, that offer homeschooling materials (worksheets, stories, activities, crafts, and coloring pages that embrace various traditions) that will provide guidance and inspiration, including these:

Broomstix, http://broomstix.blogspot.com

Friends of Rupert, http://www.friends-of-rupert.webs.com

Little Pagan Acorns, http://www.littlepaganacorns.com

Magical Child Books, http://www.magicalchildbooks.com

Pooka Pages, http://www.pookapages.com

Sources

Campanelli, Pauline and Dan. Wheel of the Year. St. Paul, MN: Llewellyn Publications, 1993.

Csikszentmihalyi, Mihaly. Flow: The Psychology of Optimal Experience. New York: Harper Perennial Modern Classics, 1990.

Kaplan-Williams, Strephon. The Jungian-Senoi Dreamwork Manual. Berkeley, CA: Journey Press, 1985.

Murdock, Maureen. Spinning Inward. Boston, MA: Shambhala Publications, 1987.

When she's not on the road or chasing free-range hens, **Natalie Zaman** is trying to figure out the universe. She is the co-author of the Graven Images Oracle deck (Galde Press) and the YA novels Sirenz and Sirenz Back in Fashion (Flux) and Blonde Ops (St. Martin's Press). Her work has appeared in Llewellyn's Magical Almanac, FATE, SageWoman, and newWitch magazines, and she currently writes the recurring feature "Wandering Witch" for Witches & Pagans magazine. Find Natalie online at http://nataliezaman.com, or at http://broomstix.blogspot.com, a collection of crafts, stories, ritual, and art she curates for Pagan families.

Illustrator: Jennifer Hewitson

Magical Transformations

Everything Old Is New Again

Prosperity Magick and the Goddess Abundantia: Create and Work with Money Altars

Najah Lightfoot

The goddess Abundantia is known as a lesser goddess in the Roman pantheon. Even so, the Romans honored her by placing her face on their coins. It is said that when she is with you, you will find coins in your path, as she spills them from her golden cornucopia of abundance.

Abundantia is a benevolent goddess who grants wishes of prosperity to those who call upon her. You can feel her presence in increased opportunities and blessings of wealth, health, and prosperity. These opportunities may show up as job interviews, or bills unexpectedly paid, or an increase in vitality, all of which are sure signs of increased prosperity.

When I work with this goddess, I time my prayers to the cycles of the waxing moon. When the moon is in the waxing phase, it is time to perform works of increase.

In the tradition of Conjure, we work with altars. In keeping with this tradition, I keep a permanent money altar in my home. When the first sliver of the waxing crescent moon appears in the sky, I stand before my money altar, light my candle to Goddess Abundantia, and say my prayers.

I find lighting a candle and praying first thing in the morning, before the sun rises in the east, to be the most beneficial of times. Night is slowly fading away, and you can feel the hope of a brand-new day. What better time could there be to commune with your goddess than the early hours of a new day?

You do not need to construct a money altar to light and work a money candle. However, in the tradition of Conjure, an altar is highly recommended. Having an altar keeps your attention focused on your work, and it also builds strong energy as you continually work it over time.

Having an altar keeps your attention focused on your work, and it also builds strong energy as you continually work it over time.

My money altar faces south. I like using the power of fire and south energy to enhance my money altar workings. It is also the direction in which most of my plants grow successfully. Since we are working with growing and increasing prosperity, as well as the color green for wealth, this area works best for me. Use your intuition or a feng shui session to determine which direction will be best for your money altar.

Constructing a Money Altar

I constructed my money altar using the following items. These are simply ideas, and you may use whatever works best for you. However, following in the tradition of Conjure, several of these items have a long history of bringing prosperity into one's life:

Lodestone: A lodestone is a magnetic piece of ore. It is used for attraction magick.

Lodestone grit: This is finely ground magnetic lodestone. It is sprinkled on top of the lodestone.

Gold flakes: These are usually found in rock shops. They normally come in a small bottle filled with water. They symbolize wealth.

Green money pyramid candle: This represents the pyramid on the back of a dollar bill.

Green and gold fabric: These are the colors of wealth and prosperity, and the fabric makes your altar look nice.

Real money and coins: These are offerings of faith that prosperity will come to you.

Petition papers: These are writings of your intention for prosperity.

Chinese rat statue: In Chinese culture, rats are used as symbols of opportunity and prosperity. The rat also corresponds to the Western astrological symbol of Gemini.

Baby from a New Orleans king cake: You'll have to eat the king cake to get the baby!

Pyrite: This mineral is also known as fool's gold.

Candle holder: Use this as a place holder for your Goddess Abundantia candle.

Whiskey: Use this to anoint the lodestone.

Green and gold glitter: Sprinkle this on the green candle.

Success Oil, Money Drawing Oil, Prosperity Oil: These oils are available at spiritual supply companies. I personally recommend Lucky Mojo (luckymojo.com) and Serpent's Kiss Magick Shop & Botanica (serpents-kiss.com). Both companies are located in California, as well as online, and they ship worldwide. You may also find that your local metaphysical store makes their own brand of these oils. If you cannot obtain these oils, you may use virgin olive oil as a substitute.

Green candle: I prefer to work with tall seven-day, glass-enclosed candles, but you can use tealights, votives, knob candles, tapers, or whichever type of candle works best for you. A Witch should always feel free to improvise! Whatever type of candle you use, you will need to dress and fix the candle before placing it on your money altar.

Florida Water: This is readily available in any metaphysical store or botanica. Use it to cleanse your candle before anointing it.

Carving tool: Use this to carve words and symbols into your candle.

Now that you have gathered all your items for your money altar, it is time to set it up. Lay down your cloths and place your items. We are magickal creatures, so trust your intuition and let it guide you on where best to place your altar items. If you work with pendulums, you may also use your pendulum to confirm that you have placed each item in just the "right" spot. Once you begin to work your money altar on a consistent basis, you may find that, as the energy grows and increases with your altar, other items will be added to it that are special only to you.

Dressing and Fixing Candles

Next we will dress and fix our candle. What do I mean by "dressed and fixed"? For my magickal craft I am trained in the ways of Conjure. "Dressed and fixed" is a Conjure term. For our purposes, we are using Conjure as it was practiced by African-American slaves, Native Americans, and European peasants, who mainly resided in the Southern states of the United States. If your mind is thinking New Orleans or Appalachian Mountains, you are on the right track.

"Dressed and fixed" means the candle has been loaded with herbs and oils, sprinkled with glitter, and prayed over and sealed for the intention for which it was created.

To dress and fix your candle, gather your green candle, Florida Water, anointing oils, gold and green glitter, and carving tool.

The candle must first be cleansed before it can be used for work. To cleanse your candle, you will use the Florida Water. If you are using a taper candle, start in the middle, washing your candle up, then down, with the Florida Water. Visualize washing away any negative energies and anyone's energies that may have come in contact with the candle.

If you are using a glass-enclosed candle, wipe the inside of the glass, the rim of the glass, and the top of the candle with Florida Water. If you are using a tealight, wipe the top of the candle with Florida Water.

Next take your carving tool and carve your name and any symbols of power and prosperity that have meaning to you into the candle.

We will now anoint the candle. Gather your Success Oil, Money Drawing Oil, Prosperity Oil, and/or olive oil. You may use one oil or a drop of each oil. If you are using a taper candle, place a drop of oil around the middle of the candle, then around the top of the candle, and finally around the bottom of the candle. Using the words "As above, so below," draw the oil up from the middle to the top of the candle, and then from the middle to the bottom of the candle. If you are using a seven-day, glass-enclosed candle, take your carving tool and poke seven holes around the edge of the candle. Next, drop seven drops of your chosen oil onto the holes in the candle, again saying "As above, so below" while you anoint the candle. Use the same procedure if you are using a tealight.

Now that your candle has been dressed, it is time to fix it. Stating your intention for increased prosperity aloud, knock three times on the candle and then tap the candle three times on a hard surface. Your candle is now dressed and fixed and ready to be placed upon the money altar.

Place your candle on the money altar. If you are using a green pyramid candle, you may anoint it as well, as previously described. The green pyramid candle can be lit or it can be used as a stationary item on the money altar.

Final Altar Steps

Sprinkle the magnetic sand on the lodestone. Pour a little whiskey on the lodestone and take a sip for yourself.

Anoint the four corners of the altar with the oil(s) you used to anoint the candle. Also place a drop of anointing oil in the center of the altar.

Recite Goddess Abundantia's prayer. The author of this prayer is unknown. I thank the author for these powerful, beautiful words:

Prayer to Goddess Abundantia

Beautiful Goddess Abundantia, I desire to be like you, carefree and filled with faith that my supply is already met, in all ways. Help me replace any money worries with joy and gratitude. Help me open my arms so that Heaven may easily help me. Thank you for all your guidance, gifts, and protection. I am truly grateful, and I am abundantly joyful and fulfilled. I let go and relax in the sure knowledge that I'm completely taken care of immediately, now, and in the future.

You may also write out this prayer and place it on the money altar.

Your money altar may become a place where others may place their prayers, petitions, and intentions as well. You may find yourself working prayers on behalf of others, enlisting the aid and benevolence of

Goddess Abundantia. She is definitely a "pay it forward" goddess. As she blesses your prosperity works and helps bring them into manifestation, you may naturally find yourself sharing her magick with others.

I believe these works have been successful because we are living in a time of resurgence of the Goddess and magickal practices. Any time we sincerely enlist prayers to the divine feminine, we are placing good energy into the world. As we live in a culture and society that is dominated by patriarchy, working with the divine feminine brings much needed balance to our world. She desires to be remembered and addressed. How wonderful it is to remember and work with this aspect of the divine mother goddess.

All hail Goddess Abundantia, from whom the brightest of blessings flow! May all your works be successful ones!

RESOURCES

"Abundantia," *Roman and Greek Gods*, http://www.talesbeyondbelief.com/roman-gods/abundantia.htm.

Virtue, Doreen, PhD. *Goddess Guidance Oracle Cards*. Carlsbad, CA: Hay House, 2004.

Najah Lightfoot *is a Priestess of the Goddess. She keeps her faith strong by following the Pagan Wheel of the Year. She is dedicated to keeping the Old Ways while living in these modern times. Najah has a passion for writing, ritual, magick, movies, and martial arts. She can be found online at www.craftandconjure.com, www.facebook.com/priestessnajah, and twitter.com/Priestess_Najah.*

Illustrator: Christa Marquez

Ready for the Reaping: Considerations for Pagan Death and Dying

Eli Effinger-Weintraub

I've chosen a dress and a wrap, in case it gets chilly or I don't look quite right. I know how I want to do my hair. I've decided against makeup unless I look particularly a fright. I've even picked out a couple places where we might go.

I've got a date with the Reaper. So do you. So does everyone we know. The only thing we don't know is when. It behooves us to make what preparations we can now, because one thing we know about this paramour is that ze loves spontaneity.

Preplanning

Some pre-death planning makes sense for everyone. Wills, medical directives and powers of attorney, password lists, and choice of funeral home (if any) are important considerations for all people, regardless of spiritual tradition. No matter what you believe about what happens to your essence or soul after death, talking to your families and communities about what you want done with your physical remains and possessions is crucial. Other matters may be particular to those of us in Pagan traditions or may need to be handled differently by our communities.

Wills can be specific or general, depending on the person writing them. One person might write page upon page, listing recipients for each of their possessions. Another may make a few bequests and instruct an executor to distribute everything else as they see fit.

No matter which method you choose for your "mundane" possessions, the people you leave behind may benefit immensely from detailed instructions regarding your magical effects. Should your tools go to your current coven or a previous one? Do your students get your Book of Shadows, or should they burn and bury it? This can be especially helpful if your executor or relatives aren't Pagan and suddenly find themselves faced with a home full of magical and spiritual books and tools whose significance they don't understand. If you have specific requirements for the disposition of your magical effects, a magical will is the place to list them.

Magical wills needn't just be about material possessions. What will become of any students you have? If you lead a coven or grove, who might you like to take over for you? List it now or forever hold your peace. If you're not out of the broom closet with your family of origin, now may be the time to discuss the matter with them, if you can. Taking time now to have these conversations, though they may be difficult, may prevent a lot of pain and confusion after you're gone.

At Death

If you are fortunate enough to receive advance warning that Death is coming for you or a beloved, you may choose to have a psychopomp or death midwife help you on your journey. Many traditions believe that the recently deceased require trained guides to free them from earthly life and see them to the afterlife, or at least to a sort of way station where a death deity or spirit will collect their souls. Regardless of your beliefs about what comes after this life, you may find comfort in having someone with you when it ends, or in knowing that someone beloved to you had someone with them.

Being a psychopomp can be difficult work and is an endeavor that shouldn't be undertaken lightly. If your community is fortunate enough to have an experienced psychopomp or death midwife, make use of their expertise. If not, consider asking someone whose maturity and magical abilities you respect if they are willing to undertake training to be able to aid you or your beloved. Whomever you choose, talk with them about your beliefs about the afterlife to make sure that, if your views and theirs are different, they can set aside their own filters and give you the death you seek. Discuss which of your loves ones you would like to have in the room with you when the time comes—and make sure those people know as well.

Just as babies are sometimes born in the back of a cab, so Death often arrives at an inconvenient time. If that happens, you or a beloved may have to decide whether it's preferable to be guided by someone without training or experience, or to trust that your soul can figure out on its own where it's supposed to go.

After Death: Practical Considerations

When someone dies, we have a bit more time to breathe, ground, and center than we tend to allow ourselves, but several things must be done fairly quickly:

- Washing and dressing the body

- Obtaining the death certificate and other necessary paperwork (in the United States, these requirements are decided by the state; know the law for your area beforehand!)

- Making arrangements for disposition and funeral or memorial services

The order in which things are done depends on whether the process is family-directed or handled professionally. In a home-directed process, family and community members, chosen beforehand, usually wash and dress the body *before* contacting the authorities. If a professional funeral director will be handling most or all aspects of the process, they will be contacted first to set the necessary procedures in motion.

The family-directed funeral community ("family," in this case, meaning all those who loved the deceased person, not just family of origin) speaks of the continuum of family and professional involvement. You might build your own coffin but hire a hearse to carry it to the cemetery. Your family might wash and dress your body before having your vigil and funeral at the funeral home. There's no one right way to arrange a family-directed funeral.

Funerals and Memorial Services

Members of many Pagan traditions find themselves in the unique position of needing to create funeral and memorial rites from scratch or trying to re-create ancient rituals with little source material to reference. This puts us in a position both enviable and terrifying—enviable because we may have the freedom to create any manner of ceremony we wish for ourselves or our loved ones, and terrifying for the same reason.

What aspects of other funerals have resonated with you? Is there particular music that always cheers you up, or a poem you reread over and over? Whatever helps you work with your grief and begin to heal may help your survivors as well.

As you consider your own funeral service or one for a beloved, it's good to bear in mind that funerals are for the bereaved as much as the deceased. You may end up needing to plan multiple rites: one for your Pagan community and one for your family of origin, co-workers, and non-Pagan friends. Keep cultural sensitivity in mind as well; another culture's funerary practice might appeal, but without cultural context and proper, respectful handling, that appropriation could leave a bad last impression on everyone.

Disposition

Spiritual beliefs and cultural traditions heavily influence many people's choice of final disposition. Does veneration of your ancestors call you to interment in a family plot or vault? Do you believe your body must be burned to free the soul within? If stepping gently upon the earth is part of your practice in life, you may wish to consider the environmental impact of your body's final disposition after death:

Conventional Burial

This is the least environmentally conscious form of disposition. Modern Western burial involves embalming the corpse, sealing it in a heavy-duty metal casket, and encasing it all in a concrete vault either above or below ground. The only upside of conventional burial is that it is allowed in the vast majority of cemeteries.

CREMATION

For many years, cremation was the only alternative to conventional burial, and the only option for folks who wanted to go out greener. Taking the body to the crematory and watching the physical form burn away can be a beautiful and healing process for our loved ones, and distributing cremains or bone fragments allows us to keep a piece of our beloved in the most literal sense. Although this method avoids the chemicals and excess of conventional burial, the cremation process releases trace amounts of mercury into the atmosphere and requires a goodly amount of fuel for the furnace.

ALKALINE HYDROLYSIS

A relatively new form of disposition is alkaline hydrolysis (also known as *resummation*, or "flameless cremation"), which uses water and an alkaline solution to dissolve the body's soft tissues, leaving the bones behind, as in cremation. Some think of this as a gentler form of disposition, perhaps suited to those who felt an affinity to the element of water. The process has a smaller environmental footprint than cremation, but the alkaline solution is currently only produced in one place in the United States. So unless you live in that region, calculation of the environmental impact must factor in transportation.

GREEN BURIAL

This is interment directly in the ground, without embalming or a vault. Sometimes the body is placed in a biodegradable coffin made of untreated wood or cardboard, and sometimes it is wrapped in a

shroud of natural fiber. The body and any covering around it degrade quickly, returning to the earth and becoming once more a part of the blessed cycle of decay and regeneration. Unfortunately, not every cemetery allows green burial.

With any full-body disposition, it's vital to talk with cemetery management beforehand to ascertain what they do and don't allow for graveside services and permanent memorials, policies around vaults and embalming, and general attitudes toward Pagan communities. In many cases, the only barrier is a perceived lack of interest. I can't count the number of times our local green burial community has been told, upon asking about a cemetery's green burial policy, "We don't have one, because no one's ever asked for one."

Looking Ahead

As our Pagan and magical communities continue to grow and evolve, we will deal with more deaths of our members and face our own inevitable passing. I was drawn to this work after encountering death in local Pagan communities that caught the survivors on the wrong foot. Not having a funeral liturgy in place—either a personal rite created by the deceased and their loved ones before death, or a standard service common to the community—they were forced to fall back on either a hastily reworded version of the monotheistic funerals of the deceased's family of origin or a completely secular service that didn't reflect their beloved's beliefs and practices.

Do you feel a call to do this work? Does your deity or Deepest Self beckon you to join with others in your tradition or community to create rituals for funerals and times of passing that can be easily adapted whenever your community faces death? Do you resonate with the idea of forming or joining a "death committee" of people with experience in death midwifery, aftercare, and logistical coordination that your community can call upon when the need arises?

The communities of Witches, Pagans, and magic workers are living in a time of great need and great opportunity. We need folks to step forward and claim roles as psychopomps and death midwives, folks willing to address both the spiritual and the physical aspects of death and dying. And we have the opportunity to create beautiful, meaningful, and healing rites for our dead and dying. Committing ourselves to honoring death will bring us all more fully into life.

Resources for Further Exploration

Funeral Consumers Alliance (FCA). A nonprofit organization dedicated to protecting a consumer's right to choose a meaningful, dignified, affordable funeral. Contains downloadable copies of the state chapters from Lisa Carlson and Joshua Slocum's website *Final Rights*, detailing end-of-life laws in each state. www.funerals.org.

Get Your Shit Together! A comprehensive, no-nonsense site for organizing the things your loved ones will need after your death. http://getyour shittogether.org.

Green Burial Council. An independent, tax-exempt, nonprofit organization working to encourage environmentally sustainable death care and the use of burial as a new means of protecting natural areas. www.green burialcouncil.org.

My Final Wishes. A fill-in-the-blanks workbook for you to record your preferences for end of life and afterward. Created by, and available from, the Threshold Care Circle of Viroqua, Wisconsin. www.thresholdcare circle.org/resources/my-final-wishes.

National Home Funeral Alliance. A nonprofit membership organization committed to reconnecting to our heritage, empowering families to care for their own, and encouraging those who further the practice of home funerals. www.homefuneralalliance.org.

The Pagan Book of Living and Dying: Practical Rituals, Prayers, Blessings, and Meditations on Crossing Over, by Starhawk, M. Macha NightMare, and the Reclaiming Collective. HarperSanFrancisco, 1997.

Undertaken With Love: A Home Funeral Guide for Congregations and Communities. Although written with Abrahamic congregations in mind, this downloadable booklet is easily adapted to Pagan communities and contains a wealth of information about preparing, physically and emotionally, for death in your community. http://undertakenwithlove.org.

Eli Effinger-Weintraub *is a naturalistic Reclaiming-tradition witch rooted in the Twin Cities watershed. Her work has appeared in print in* Witches & Pagans, Circle Magazine, *and* The Shining Cities *and on stages around the United States. Eli tweets sporadically as @awflyweeeli.*

Illustrator: Kathleen Edwards

Pansexuality and Paganism

Melanie Marquis

As modern Pagans, most of us enjoy a religious practice that is free from discrimination based on gender or sexual orientation. In fact, it's often this openness and tolerance that initially attracts newcomers to our community. Seeing beyond the physical form, seeing beneath the surface in order to find the true heart of the experience, is second nature to many Pagans due to our familiarity with the magickal arts, and it's also a core element of pansexuality. By examining the connections between pansexuality and Paganism, you'll gain a greater understanding of how these

Pansexuals like who they want to like, regardless of whether that person is a man, woman, hermaphrodite, or transgendering person in the midst of transition— they simply don't consider gender to be an important criterion when choosing a mate.

shared concepts can be used to help break through limiting factors in your life as well as in your magick.

You might be wondering, just what in the world is pansexuality, anyway? Don't feel too out of the loop if you haven't heard the word before. It's a fairly recent term used to describe the idea of sexual attraction and romantic love regardless of gender. Synonymous terms you may have heard include "gender-blind" and "omnisexual." Pansexuals like who they want to like, regardless of whether that person is a man, woman, hermaphrodite, or transgendering person in the midst of transition—they simply don't consider gender to be an important criterion when choosing a mate.

Pansexuality is connected with Paganism in several ways: through androgynous deities, through seeing beauty beyond form, and through a refusal to accept false limitations. Let's take a deeper look at these commonalities, then we'll consider some ways to use this information to expand and enrich your own magickal practice.

The Divine Androgynous

While androgyny—having both male and female qualities, or an ambiguous gender identity or sexual orientation—is not the same thing as pansexuality, there's clearly a lot of common ground between the two concepts. Both androgyny and pansexuality dissolve the idea of strict, limiting gender identities, and both also illuminate the fact that feminine and masculine energies are always intertwined, always interacting and connecting, and are never truly separated. They are two sides of the same coin, and not one of us nor anything else on earth has just one side or the other.

Our tendency to want to label energies as "masculine" or "feminine" serves the purposes of classification and personification, but it can be limiting. The reason behind personifying deity in the first place is to make it easier for people to relate to the Divine—but if you're not personally restricted by gender roles, thinking of deities in terms of male and female isn't going to help you feel any closer to them. While androgynous deities are generally described as illustrating polarities or unions, they also serve the purpose of providing a personified godform with which gender-blind individuals can potentially connect and relate.

Androgynous deities are found all over the world. From the Egyptian Hapi to the Greek Hermaphroditus to the Hindu Ardhanarishvara, gods with ambiguous or combined gender identities abound. Working with these energies in magickal practice can help the Witch to see beyond gender-based restrictions and expectations, regardless of the Witch's personal gender identity and sexual

orientation. You don't have to be androgynous or pansexual to work with androgynous deities. It's not about changing who you are or pretending to be something you're not; it's about expanding the limits of who you can be and what you can do. Working with androgynous energies can help you to realize those full potentials.

Seeing Beauty Beyond Form

In magick as well as pansexuality, beauty is found beyond the outward form, illuminated and activated through the liberating power of love. When a Witch sets out to cast a spell, they're aware of the potential that lies beyond and beneath surface appearances. Circumstances might look difficult, but with a little love-powered magick, the Witch can find the heart of the matter and transform it into a more desirable form. Similarly, when a pansexual person sets out to find love or sensual pleasure, they're aware of the potential beauty that lies within the *spirit* of the individual, regardless of outward gendered form.

With love, it's the heart that matters, and this heart can truly transform even the "ugliest" bodies into works of art. Now, this is not to imply that pansexuals aren't selective. They can be just as selective as anyone else, only they don't use gender as a deciding factor. There are naturally more options, however, in both magick and love when there's an understanding that everyone deserves love and that anyone can be beautiful. We feel this when we're in circle, experiencing a ritual with our comrades—gender doesn't matter, age doesn't matter, sexual orientation doesn't matter, appearance doesn't matter. We are Witches, standing together as humans for the common cause of affecting the world through magick. Why should it be any different when we look for love and life and pleasure in the world at large? Why should gender restrictions matter sometimes but not other times? If we can see the beauty of one another when we're working magick together, why would that beauty become invisible once the robes come off and the outward form is revealed? Beauty comes from within, and both Pagans and pansexuals tend to be extraordinarily good at seeing that.

No More False Limitations

We Witches don't take "No, you can't, that's not possible" as an answer, and neither do pansexuals. We know that with love, anything is possible, and we refuse to restrict our loving actions based on societal expectations or religious beliefs with which we disagree. In both pansexuality and Pagan magickal practice, we set our own limits, defining our own expectations of what we want, what we deserve, and who we can be. The world is always telling us what we can do and what we can't do—but we are the world, and it's up to each one of us to decide just what sort of world we'd like to create. By finding new ways of incorporating pansexuality into rituals, you can bust through even more of those illusory boundaries and limitations, in your magick as well as in your life.

Pansexuality in Ritual and Magick

Pansexuality is already a part of many of our rituals and magickal workings. Any time our magick or ritual transcends the restrictions and expectations of gender-based identity, elements of pansexuality are at play. If you'd like to explore further, you might start by asking yourself some questions: Do you feel your magick tends to take on a certain flavor or focus on certain goals due to your gender identity? Are you placing any needless restrictions on yourself, as a loving, sensual being or as a Witch? How might you move past these boundaries by expanding your perception beyond your own gender identity?

You might decide to give an entire ritual a pansexual theme, invoking androgynous deities or ritually shedding or shifting gender identities for the course of the ceremony. As another option, you might do a ritual that has as its main focus something other than pansexuality, but incorporate pansexual elements as a tool for energy raising and magickal power magnification. Pansexual magick works especially well for magick intended to transform, remove obstacles, or unite disparate energies, so you have lots of options as to your spell goal.

Whatever the preliminary particulars of your ritual, when it comes time to raise the energy and magnify the power that's been collecting in the sacred space, have everyone gather in the middle of the circle. Begin touching one another to help raise the energy and magnify the magickal power, just as you might use drumming, dancing, or chanting to amplify energetic vibrations. This touching could take a number of forms, from platonic hugs and handshakes shared fully clothed, to skyclad sensual touching—just be sure everyone discusses, agrees on, and understands the purpose, limits, and allowances before you begin the ritual.

Whether engaging in hugs and handshakes or orgiastic revelry, try to shift your focus away from the gender identity of the people you are touching. Instead, see if you can perceive the people around you as unique fragments of the Divine, a power that transcends far beyond human ideas of man and woman. See yourself as more than your body, and allow a loving energy to pour out of your hands and into the bodies of those around you, filling them with an intense, bright power. As you are touched, enjoy the buildup of magickal energy within your body. Let the emotion build to a climax, create a clear mental vision of your intention, and then, simultaneously as a group, release the energy out of the body, directing it toward the completion of the magickal goal.

Pansexuality and Pagan Spirituality

While pansexuality may or may not be a sexual orientation with which you personally identify, as a modern Pagan, there's a good chance your practices reflect values shared by many pansexual individuals. The gender-blind ability to see the heart that beats beyond the outward form is a force of great love and great magick, able to transform obstacles into assets and turn beautiful into more beautiful. We all have our own boundaries and limitations to transcend, and both pansexuality and Paganism are paths that invite us to do just that.

Melanie Marquis *is the author of* The Witch's Bag of Tricks (Llewellyn, 2011) *and* A Witch's World of Magick (Llewellyn, 2014). *She's the founder of United Witches global coven and also serves as local coordinator for Denver Pagan Pride. She's written for many Pagan publications, including* Circle Magazine, Pentacle Magazine, *and* Spellcraft. *A freelance writer, folk artist, Tarot reader, mother, and eclectic Witch, she's passionate about finding the mystical in the mundane through personalized magick and practical spirituality. Visit Melanie at www.facebook.com/melaniemarquisauthor or www.melaniemarquis.com or on Twitter @unitedwitches.*

Illustrator: Tim Foley

Brooch, Comb, and Buckle:
A Peek at the "Real" Goths

Linda Raedisch

Have you heard of the Goths? Of course you have: there's Gothic architecture, the Gothic novel, and the Gothic hand, a calligraphic script that the Goths never used themselves. And then there are those other "goths," a recent phenomenon named after the "gothic" themes that captivate them, those themes named in turn for the blackened spires, gargoyles, and ruined abbeys that inspired the Gothic Revivalists of the Victorian era. I was aware going into this article that the ancient Goths—the "real" Goths—might be a hard people to pin down, but as the reference materials piled up around my ears, a surprising realization hit me: the Goths were a snooze.

While I'm sure it was all very exciting while it was happening, the long accounts of river crossings, internal rivalries, and endless regroupings have a soporific effect on the reader, at least on this one. What had ever led me to believe that *these* Goths might make interesting reading for Witches, Pagans, and the Goths' own latter-day namesakes? I closed the scholarly tomes and looked back at what I already knew, or thought I knew, about this shadowy force of history. I composed a list of what I considered to be the Goths' most interesting points and proceeded to hold their feet to the fire. What follows are the results of my interrogations, with each preconceived notion appearing in italics. You might share some of them. If so, and if you are romantically attached to any of them, consider yourself warned. Rest assured, however, that for each notion of which I am about to cruelly disabuse you, I will offer up at least one engaging truth.

The Goths were a Scandinavian people who crossed the Baltic Sea from Sweden and then proceeded in an orderly fashion to what is now Ukraine. This version of Gothic origins was widely accepted until quite recently. While those early Goths did eventually fetch up at the shores of the Black Sea, they came in dribs and drabs, and there is no indication that they were originally from Sweden. Those who would sooner or later be known as "Goths" seem to have arisen from the Wielbark Culture of northern Poland in the early centuries CE.

Let's meet one of them, shall we? A tall woman, her long reddish brown hair is secured at the back of her head with a comb of carved antler. Spring has come to her village, and she wears a sleeveless dress of pale wool, the tightly woven fabric held together at the shoulders with T-shaped brooches. Sunlight breaking through a bank of clouds picks out the carving in the bronze buckle at her waist, touches the tools and ornaments hanging from her leather belt, and sets her necklace of amber beads to glowing. Our lady's dress falls all the way to the toes of her leather slippers, and she hitches her skirts in her hand as she makes her

way between the low, thatched houses, scattering flocks of chickens as she goes. She appears to be in a hurry. Perhaps she is late to a feast? We wave, but she does not see us; she is too busy trying to keep her slippers from the mud.

The Goths spoke an ancient form of German. Yes and no. Our Gothic friends spoke a language of the now extinct East Germanic branch. Gothic was not the ancestor of German or any living language. If, however, you were plunked down in a fifth-century Gothic settlement on the shores of the Black Sea, you might be able to pick out a word or two. Let's assume that you have been, and that you are a male and one of the fighting elite. No combs for you; you wear your long *skuft* twisted into a skein at the side of your head. Strutting about the settlement, you recognize the words *airtha*, "earth," referring to the rich soil hereabouts, and *sunno*, "sun." There's *skip* for "ship," and *wigs* for "way." Suddenly, you hear the thunder of hoofbeats coming from the east and your *frauja* bellowing at you to fetch your *skildus*, *hilms*, and *meki*. Oh, better put on your *brunjo*, too: things could get rough out there.

Gothic contained many Celtic loan words, of which the chain mail *brunjo* may have been one, while the two-edged *meki* probably came from Central Asia, along with those Huns who are about to crest the hill. Still, Gothic was first and foremost a Germanic language, and the Goths shared important aspects of their religion with other Germanic groups. The Gothic *frauja*, "lord," reminds us of the Norse god Frey, whose name also means "lord." A *frauja* was a lord in the sense of "lord of the house." The *gards*, or "house," included not just a roof and four walls but everyone in and around them: family members, retainers, servants, and slaves. *Gards* could also refer to the *garden*, the fields beyond, and even the world we live in. The Goths' *Midjungards* corresponds to the Norse *Midgard* and thence to Tolkien's Middle Earth.

The Wielbarkian lady whom we observed hurrying along the muddy *wigs* back in Poland may have been bound for a feast at which meat was consecrated to the gods and then consumed by all members of the community, just as sacred horsemeat was solemnly passed round in Scandinavia during the Viking Age. The Amals, a ruling family of the Goths, believed themselves to be descended from the Ansis, sky gods whom we can safely equate with the Norse Aesir, so if you don't make it through the coming battle, you might soon find yourself in some Gothic version of Valhalla.

The Gothic cathedrals are reflections of the forest groves in which ancient Germanic tribesmen worshiped their gods. Gothic architecture actually evolved from the squat and stolid Romanesque, the change spurred by a yearning for light inside these massive structures. Gothic cathedrals are identifiable by their pointed arches, delicate traceries of brick or stone, and expanses of colored glass. "Gothic" architecture did not receive that label until the very end of the Gothic era, and then it was used not as a compliment but in the sense of "barbaric." Not everyone loves gargoyles!

And then again, Gothic architecture is much more organic, much "folkier," than the Romanesque or any movement that followed. Typically, the plans for the cathedral were dreamed up (sometimes literally) by a cleric, then executed by a succession of master masons, glass-cutters and stone-carvers, each bringing his own personal visions—and nightmares—to the project. If a little of that old Pagan forest grove still lingered in the collective memory of the artisans, it would certainly have been imparted to the cathedral.

The Goths were a distinct people. Textbooks like to divide the Goths into two main categories: Ostrogoths (Goths of the East) and Visigoths (Goths of the West). Actually, the name *Ostrogoths* carried the connotation of "People of the Rising Sun," while the term *Visigoth* was made up out of whole cloth by a Roman writer to describe those Goths who had oozed into parts of Italy, France, and Spain. In addition to those Ostrogoths and Visigoths, there were also Burgundians, Gepids, Langobards, Greuthungi, and Tervingi, all of whom were numbered at one time or another among the Goths. Some Goths were actually Huns, while some Huns were actually Goths who had adopted the customs of taking broken mirrors and footed cauldrons with them into their graves as well as binding the skulls of their infants so they might grow up into handsome coneheads.

Often, Gothicness was a matter of ambition or circumstance as much as birth. It's possible that, by the fifth century, only the aristocracy were considered to be full-on Goths. When they first started to elbow their way into the Roman Empire, the Romans declined to intermarry with them, not because the Goths were Pagans—they had not been for some time—but because they were Arian Christians rather than Roman Catholics. For a little while, this distinction helped to maintain the Goths' own ethnic identity, but eventually they all became Catholics.

The Goths had cool names. This one is absolutely true. Here is a random sampling, which I hope expectant parents will find useful.

For the girls, we have Amalasuntha, Amalafrida ("peace of the Amals"), Sunigilda, Ranilda, and Stafara. This last was inscribed inside a gold finger ring found in a treasure hoard in Italy.

You'll be forgiven for mistaking Valamir, Thiudimir, and Vidimir for Stewards of Gondor in Middle Earth; they were in fact members of the Ostrogothic Amal Dynasty. Visigothic heavies include Alaric, Frideric, Himnerith, and Chindaswinth. One of the most famous Goths of all, Wulfila, who translated the Bible into Gothic, was technically not a Goth at all but the child of captured Cappadocian Christians. His name, which is indeed Gothic, means "little wolf."

The Huns were the children of evil spirits and banished Gothic Witches.
Well, I never really believed this one, but I wondered how much
credence the Goths themselves gave to this slur. Was it the inven-
tion of the Gothic historian Jordanes, who claimed to have gotten
it from an earlier source? And who exactly were these Witches?
Jordanes calls them *Haliurunnae*, which translates roughly as "nec-
romancers." The whole scandal was supposed to have occurred during the reign of the legendary King Filimer, who led the Goths into
"Scythia" in what is now Ukraine. This was prime real estate, so the
place would have already been inhabited by nomads and farmers.
This was also long before the Goths' conversion to Christianity, so
the practice of sorcery in itself would not have been grounds for
expelling a woman from the tribe. In fact, the king himself was ex-
pected to have at least a little white magic at his fingertips. So were
these Haliurunnae White Witches gone bad, or were they Witches
of another stripe entirely?

The Goths were first and foremost farmers. The whole reason for
migrating to the shores of the Black Sea was because the soil was so
much better than that of northern Poland. Like all farmers in those
days, and in the centuries to come, they would have blamed any problems with the crops or the livestock on supernatural agency. They
would no doubt have turned
to their own magical practitioners for help, and those
practitioners may well have
pointed the finger at the indigenous Witches. Archae-
ologists tell us that at this
time the region north of the
Black Sea was home to the
Zarubintsy culture. There,
in the rich river valleys, the

Zarubintsians would have performed their own rituals to ensure the fertility of their fields. Influenced on the one hand by the Celts and on the other by the Old Iranian-speaking Sarmatians, the folkways of these people may have looked strange to the newly arrived Germanic tribesmen.

Perhaps the Goths did not like the native Witches' oddly shaped cauldrons (not to mention their oddly shaped heads!) or were suspicious of their potions, which may well have been laced with cannabis. Or perhaps King Filimer was simply being sexist: according to the Greek writers, Sarmatian women were encouraged to bear arms and, in fact, swords, arrows, and scale armor have been found in many of their graves.

Jordanes tells us only that King Filimer *suspected* the Haliurunnae, not of what. He does make it clear that these women were of Filimer's own Gothic race rather than Scythian, Sarmatian, or Dacian, as one might expect. It is possible that some of the Gothic women had become warriors in the Central Asian tradition, threatening Gothic manhood in the process. Driven beyond the pale of Gothic settlement, the scorned women wandered the gloomy swamps where they encountered the "unclean spirits" with whom they conceived the troll-like Huns. The relationship between Goth and Hun was highly ambivalent. Each reviled the other, while at the same time adopting large chunks of each other's culture. Jordanes's tale is, then, a grudging acknowledgment of kinship between enemies.

· · · · · · · · · · · · ·

Well, there you have it: the Goths, as they were and as they might have been. It's clear that the historic Goths really have nothing to do with our own brooding, black-clad teens. (My apologies to any over-the-hill goths out there.) Or do they? As we have seen, being Gothic was often a matter of self-identification rather than of birth.

Gothic culture spread rapidly throughout the Roman Empire just as the goth phenomenon has spread to all corners of the developed world—witness the Japanese-created Pokémon "Gothita." If you're still feeling disenchanted, however, I offer up the Melanchlanoi as consolation. These people, who may or may not have been early Goths, were one of the many northern barbarian tribes listed by the ancient Greeks. Their name, in Greek, means "Black Mantles."

Suggested Reading

Heather, Peter. *The Goths*. Cambridge, MA: Blackwell Publishers, 1996. (A trusted sleep aid.)

Jordanes. *The Origin and Deeds of the Goths*. Translated by Charles C. Mierow. http://people.ucalgary.ca/~vandersp/Courses/texts/jordgeti.html. (Also known as the *Getica*. The Haliurunnae appear in Chapter XXIV.)

Robinson, Orrin W. *Old English and Its Closest Relatives: A Survey of the Earliest Germanic Languages*. Stanford, CA: Stanford University Press, 1992. (You and your friends will soon be chatting in Gothic over coffee.)

Todd, Malcolm. *Everyday Life of the Barbarians: Goths, Franks and Vandals*. New York: G. P. Putnam's Sons, 1972. (A good introduction to the subject.)

Wolfram, Herwig. *History of the Goths*. Translated by Thomas J. Dunlap. Berkeley, CA: University of California Press, 1988. (No beach read, but contains good information on language, religion, and lifeways.)

Linda Raedisch's *most recent book for Llewellyn is* The Old Magic of Christmas: Yuletide Traditions for the Darkest Days of the Year. *She has also written on Native American themes for the school and library market and since 2011 has been penning articles on obscure subjects for Llewellyn's annuals. Her principal interests are the spiritual and material culture of northern Europe during the pre-Christian era. She makes her home in northern New Jersey.*

Illustrator: Jennifer Hewitson

My Great-Great-Grandmother's Hair: How the Power of Language Shapes Reality

Thuri Calafia

We've come a long way, baby. Or…have we? There's no question that the feminist movement of the 1960s and 1970s helped us Pagan women get to where we are today, with our freedom to choose to love and worship goddesses instead of, or along with, our gods. Many great authors and teachers showed us that the Goddess never really died, she just switched forms, often becoming the watered-down "saints" of Christianity and sometimes even their deities, such as Mary, who has strong associations with Isis, Queen of Heaven. We learned about female power being different than, but not inferior to, male power, and that there is a place for us in the world, that our work and our contributions are important and worthy of respect.

Then what happened? Feminism kind of took a nosedive in the 1980s and hasn't really resurfaced, although, happily, the Pagan movement has continued to thrive, and within it, respect for women is still strong. Still, even with that dynamic, it's been difficult, at least for this post-feminism priestess, to come to terms with *terms* at times—the way in which we women refer to ourselves, our peers, and our deities. As a writer, I cannot deny the power of language and the effect it has on the human psyche, and as a feminist, I cannot deny that some of the words and phrases I read and hear women using about ourselves and our deities sometimes just make me scratch my head, wondering, "What's up with that?"

> **As a feminist, I cannot deny that some of the words and phrases I read and hear women using about ourselves and our deities sometimes just make me scratch my head, wondering, "What's up with that?"**

In my earliest days of goddess worship, I remember stomping across the front lawn of my home, my little nine-year-old passions fuming that someone would actually have the audacity to call the stories about the ancient Greek gods and goddesses "myths." I had just heard an adult use the word "myth," which the person then clarified for me as being the same as "falsehood." This led to a very loud and heated debate about Christianity versus, well, any belief that was other-than-Christian, and whether the latter was simply wrong, a lie.

"How can anyone possibly *know*?" I asked loudly to no one in particular, knowing that until a person dies and crosses over, those mysteries are never going to be resolved in any kind of clear or absolute manner.

As I made my way across the street and into the huge field beyond, my emotions calmed, and I began speaking to Great Artemis, my beloved matron goddess, whom I'd devoted myself to already, one hot afternoon earlier that summer. Her presence comforted and consoled me, and I took her wise counsel seriously, even then. And I felt more connected to her in many ways than I did to the woman who raised me, even then. Artemis was my goddess, my beloved matron, though I didn't have the language for it at the time. I just knew that she was everything to me, the ultimate guiding force of my life—my mother, my sister, my best friend. My goddess.

Years later, after "coming out" as Wiccan, I learned that many Pagans have matron goddesses and patron gods, and that these connections are deeply personal, sacred. I had sort of rediscovered the divine feminine through a lesbian support group and had put the whole idea of male deity on the back burner for a while, and didn't worry so much about whether I had a patron god or not. I did discover him, or I guess I should say "them," years later, after my other matron goddesses came to me, and have had close connections with several gods and goddesses ever since.

Never, however, had I heard of a person's closest personal female deity referred to as a "patron" until fairly recently. I was at a Pagan family picnic, here in my new home in the Portland, Oregon, metro area. A woman I'd just met made some reference to her "patron goddess Brigit," and I thought to myself, "That is wrong on so many levels," as I'd been taught that, first of all, Brigit is the name of the saint that the Celtic goddess Brighid (correctly pronounced "breed") was Christianized to become, and wow, did this woman *actually* just refer to her most beloved female deity as *a guy*? I didn't want to be rude, either by correcting another priestess, especially in public, or by interrupting her discourse, so I just listened politely, nodded my head, and tried not to go all…twitchy.

See, while it's certainly true that the idea of "patronage" started way back in early Greece and Rome, and that it had to do with supporting, fostering, or protecting a person or thing, there's no escaping the very real etymology of the word; it still has its roots in the Old French, and still, first and foremost, means "*father*"! Remember, too, that after the fall of Troy, Greece became very patriarchal and misogynistic, so the only persons considered *capable* of such support and fosterage were men. And although the word, even in today's dictionaries, is defined primarily as this spirit of generosity and support, if you look a little farther down the page, you will see the rather diluted "patron*ess*" (italics mine) describing "a female

patron," thereby proving beyond a shadow of a doubt that the word "patron" clearly and unequivocally means "male." The word "matron," on the other hand, also has its roots in the Old French, and describes "a married woman," "a mother," or a "woman of established age and dignity," all of which clearly point to the female. And if anyone has ever had a mother who cared about them, they will agree that a woman, especially in these modern times, can most certainly be just as capable of supporting, fostering, or helping a person grow as a man can. And protection? Ever seen a mama bear?

In spite of all this, you will hear folks in the Pagan community using the phrase "My patron goddess..." alarmingly often! Again we must consider the power of language and give some thought as to what we are saying, as words create energy, and energy creates *reality*. Take a moment and think about the woman who gave birth to you. Is that woman your *father*? Would you walk up to her and say, "Hey, *Dad*"? For a community that prides itself on good scholarship, and which is often more inquisitive about the status quo than the average person, and which claims to *honor the power of the female*, it's rather odd to me that we so often trip over our own words, so to speak, when referring to the female. But when you consider the fact that we are still products of our culture and that our culture is still pretty confused when it comes to women and how to deal with our very unique and yet very real power, it's not surprising we get tangled up in language, sometimes interminably.

Take the words "goddess" and "priestess," for example. Years ago, when I told a boss of mine that I needed the day off to perform a wedding ceremony, he smiled and said, "Oh, I didn't know you were a priest!" I smiled back, and with my best, most "priestessly" manners, said, "Well, I'm a priestess of the goddess, yes." I Googled the word "priestess" for this article and, interestingly enough, found the definition as "a female priest of a non-Christian religion." Hmm, so it's all about *who we worship* and not about who we are, then, eh? What is up with that? It reminds me of the time of my nephew's birth when my brother jokingly told his girlfriend on the phone, "My sister had a boy, so I'm an uncle, not an aunt." Still, I have to admit, and I think many female-identified Pagans would agree, that even though we learn in beginner-level English classes that prefixes and suffixes "weaken" words, it feels right and good that we refer to ourselves as *priestesses* and our female deities as *goddesses*. Likewise, in Western culture, we're pretty used to the words "waitress," "stewardess," and "actress."

But what about the words to which we add that "-ess" suffix less commonly or less often? I must admit that the first time I ever heard a metaphysical shop owner say she was the "proprietress," I about came apart. It just sounded…*wrong*, somehow, like she was diminishing her own status of ownership by making it sound all "girly." I mean, would she have called herself the "owner-ess"? I literally had to bite the insides of my cheeks to keep from laughing, because she was flippin' *serious*! I mean, who says that, really? "Sculptress" sounds pretty strange, too, and what about "authoress"? Even stranger. I've actually had folks refer to me in this way, and let me tell you, I usually find myself wanting to say, "No, I'm an *actual* author, not an 'author-ess,' okay?" Most of these "-ess" words just don't sound like real words to me somehow, or at least not like words belonging to people one would take seriously. I remember a long time ago, when I was a kid, I was watching some game show, and this woman was describing her work. She said she was a nanny, and she lived in a house with "four children, one adult, and one 'adultress.'" The crowd roared with laughter. So we can see how sometimes even the meaning of words can change when we add this "-ess" suffix to them. Certainly our perception of them does.

Going from the sublime to the ridiculous, I can remember my early days of ardent feminism, when I and the women in my support groups all felt it was vitally important to remove the male-sounding roots from as many words as possible, so "women" became "wimmin," "woman" became "womyn," and "history" became "herstory." This all made a great deal of sense to us back then, and even today, many women struggle to find words to describe ourselves and our experience in a way that honors and respects our uniqueness as individuals, rather than lumping us into language roles that are just part of the same homogenous group as our male counterparts. But is this necessary? Moreover, is it respectful? How so? And to whom? And how can we, as women, as *powerful Witches*, often in leadership roles in our individual communities, find a way to take *ourselves* seriously when so much of our language is either male-centered or fluffed up with "-ess" to sound "girly"? Where do we find balance?

How can we, as women, as *powerful Witches*, often in leadership roles in our individual communities, find a way to take *ourselves* seriously when so much of our language is either male-centered or fluffed up with "-ess" to sound "girly"?

Trying to change even the simplest language structures can be like running up a hillside of smooth stone in ballet slippers. I remember trying to explain to an ex-partner of mine, years ago, that if we, as a people, were going to use any pronoun as a "generic," it should be the word "she" and not "he," because the word "she" contains both "he" and "she" within it. He looked at me, eyebrows raised, and told me in no uncertain terms that I'd better not ever call him, or any other man, "she" in his presence or I'd be sorry!

It gets even better. Unlike "heroine," a seemingly powerful way to refer to a female of legend, we now apparently also have the rather interesting "ancestress." The first time I saw the word was in a Witchvox article, in the plural form, "ancestresses." I thought, "Ohmygods, that just sounds way too much like my great-great-grandmother's *hair!*" Really? How can we take such words seriously?

But maybe all this fuss over language wouldn't even be necessary if the very core of our beliefs *truly held* that women are just as good, just as valuable, and just as important to our society as men are. Maybe better, clearer language could be born from that, in a natural and comfortable (dare I say "organic"?) process. I can see the dynamic of true equality—of *egalitarianism*—blossoming in the Pagan subculture, and it makes my heart sing with joy, although I know we're not all the way there yet. Still, it gives me hope, for I know that a person's spiritual beliefs are the foundation and core of their other beliefs, and that these beliefs dictate their actions, their choices, and, ultimately, their language. I believe that if we, as a spiritual subculture, can promote the concept and energy of egalitarianism enough, perhaps we can help make that awareness grow into the rest of the world, through actions born of love and truth in accord, through the very real and immediate power of language.

Thuri Calafia *is an ordained minister and Wiccan High Priestess, teacher, and founder of Circles School of Wicca and Witchcraft. She is the author of* Dedicant: A Witch's Circle of Fire *and* Initiate: A Witch's Circle of Water, *which are complete courses of study based on her teachings. She is currently working on the third book in the series,* Adept: A Witch's Circle of Earth. *She is actively involved in the Pagan community in the Pacific Northwest.*

Illustrator: Bri Hermanson

Making Myth Matter

Ember Grant

How many times have you called upon a deity for his or her influence in a ritual or spell? We often look to the myriad "personalities" of gods and goddesses to enhance our magical work and to give us a sense of connection to something larger than ourselves. Some Witches and Wiccans are even part of reconstruction paths that seek to rebuild a particular pantheon of deities. But, for the sake of this article, I will address the way a majority of practitioners use mythology and deity as metaphors and symbols, and how we can learn to move beyond that reference to invite a deeper understanding of mythology and what it can mean to us in our lives and our magical practice.

Why Mythology Is Important to Us

Well-known mythologist Joseph Campbell wrote prolifically about the reasons that myth matters to us. According to him, in addition to the importance of rites, there are four functions of myth: (1) to evoke a sense of awe and gratefulness; (2) to formulate an image of the cosmos; (3) to create a societal system, a shared set of rights and wrongs; and (4) a psychological function. Science and secular laws have defined our world (to a certain extent), and we have structured morals into laws that help guide our societal behavior. So that leaves numbers one and four: a sense of awe and the psychological function—the seeking of personal fulfillment.

That craving of awe and fulfillment is one reason so many of us have turned to mysticism. But, in modern times, we don't have one singular great body of myth that unites us. Many of us look to the old ways to find meaning for a connection missing in the modern world. This is most likely not nostalgia for a simpler time, but a longing for meaning. We need myths. We crave the stories and the structure for guidance, comfort, consolation, unity, and identity; for a human experience shared across the ages, to understand ourselves and our world.

As modern Pagans, we have in some ways created our own shared set of rites. We have a seasonal structure that we use to celebrate, and most of us still acknowledge various rites of passage, many that are relevant across cultures. And yet, according to *Wisdom of the Mythtellers* by Sean Kane, there is no universal myth, despite our seemingly similar human psyche.

In addition, many of the traditions in the Wiccan calendar are based on early agricultural models of life—preparing the land, planting, and harvesting. But we must remember that agriculture created a boundary between us and nature in many ways. We often overlook stories from people living with the uncertainty of nature—stories of pre-agricultural times. Or we romanticize the past as a time when people lived closer to the land. Kane's point is that we're modern, so we can't truly re-create the past and the old stories. But we can look at the patterns and why they matter. It's not that we shouldn't use the myths, but that we should look even deeper at the reasons for those stories.

Kane urges us to look at the basic relationship between people and nature, and the patterns that arise. If we compare myths across cultures, we find more than stories about gods and goddesses; we see relationships and patterns rooted in nature itself and the interaction of people with the environment. Even before people settled into an agricultural lifestyle, they recognized the patterns and rhythms of life and nature.

Kane points out that "the mythtellers speak of the powers *in relation to* each other, and with an eye to the whole ecology, not separate functions of it" (p. 34). This "knowledge of pattern is the beginning of every practical wisdom" (pp. 36–37). He points out that once people domesticated animals, the "animals stop talking in myth." We lost something when we rooted ourselves and began controlling the land. "Myths which evolve in sympathy with nature are different from myths which compete with it" (p. 22). And so, before organized religion, before agriculture, there is something deeper to consider.

As we grow as individuals, and as our societies and cultures learn and evolve, we need a system that encourages our developing consciousness, rather than keeping it within a rigid, dogmatic structure.

Institutionalized religions rarely acknowledge this process. This is why we need to find ways to apply myths to our modern lives. We are not the same people who wrote the story, even if we do share some experiences.

Finding New Meaning in Our Favorite Myths

While it's beneficial to explore a wide range of myths, we can examine familiar myths more deeply and study them for their various interpretations. Our modern lives give us the advantage to apply everything we've learned as a part of human society. This offers many different perspectives on a tale. We need to try to see beyond the story and its ties to the era in which it was created, and look to the basic pattern of human life and our relationship to the natural world. Consider the pattern of the story and how it relates to natural cycles of life, the environment, and people's basic life cycles, feelings, or instincts.

> **We can examine familiar myths more deeply… We need to try to see beyond the story and its ties to the era in which it was created, and look to the basic pattern of human life and our relationship to the natural world.**

To illustrate this point, I'll apply these steps to a well-known myth: the story of Daphne and Apollo. Remember, there are many versions of myths. I'm summarizing Ovid's version of the story.

The story begins as Apollo insults Cupid for the use of his bow, suggesting that Cupid's use of the arrow to induce love is silly and foolish, and in no way comparable to the glory of battle. So Cupid shoots Apollo and Daphne, using one arrow (a gold one) to induce love in Apollo for Daphne but using the other (made of lead) to force

the opposite feelings in her. Apollo desires her more than anything, but she is repulsed by him and flees his pursuit. Daphne prays to her father, Peneus, a river god, and he transforms her into a tree. Daphne is the Greek word for laurel, the tree she becomes, which from that moment on is considered sacred to Apollo.

Let's look at some modern interpretations of this myth. There's the obvious lesson that no one is immune to desire—Cupid proves that and punishes Apollo for his arrogance. There's a statue of Daphne and Apollo in Rome created by Bernini that has a Latin inscription on the bottom (attributed to Pope Urban VIII): "Every lover who pursues the joys of fleeing beauty fills his hands with leaves or plucks bitter berries." This adds other suggestions to the story. It can mean that pursuit of unrequited love will result in bitterness. It can also mean to beware of loving for physical beauty, because it doesn't last. So, some lessons from the story are: don't chase what doesn't want to be caught; realize that no one is immune to feelings—don't be arrogant in the face of love; and pray to nature for relief—nature can be an escape.

I've distilled the essence down into these brief lessons, but there are many more ways to examine it. One can also look to Daphne's point of view as seeking release from a relationship that won't work—feeling like she is being hunted or pressured. There can be both a literal and symbolic retreat.

Remember, too, that the Daphne story has alternately been interpreted as attempted "rape" and as love or passion. In some studies, these stories are not considered actual rape but rather a ravishing—a feeling of overwhelming emotion. You can look at it both ways. The root of the story is not that Apollo is trying to capture or harm Daphne, but that Cupid forced it because Apollo insulted him, implying he was somehow immune to feelings of love (remember, Apollo was all about reason and temperance—no excess). This was a punishment for him, a taste of what he was certain he could resist.

Another lesson could be to seek help to accept what one has or cannot have, to heal, or to recognize feelings.

In addition, if we consider the culture of the ancient Greeks, we learn that one word for "wife" was *damar*, which means "tamed." Dr. Elizabeth Vandiver explores this in her lectures on classical mythology. In this context, we might view Daphne as a woman who didn't want to be domesticated—she wanted to remain wild and free. Like the goddess Artemis (Apollo's twin sister), who was a virgin because, we can guess, she rejected being dominated by a man, perhaps we can extend this to Daphne. She became a tree to escape Apollo's grasp. She wanted to be wild—in this case, unclaimed by a man—independent.

Now, looking deeper for core patterns, we can see the issue of lust and desire—the basic cycle of life and reproduction, the urge to mate. Cupid personifies our feelings of love toward others. We must not forget how we are programmed to seek what we desire and that we have a basic need to satisfy our physical desire for another person.

Next, to address the human interaction with nature, consider the tree. Trees were part of the environment before humans. We evolved with them around us. They inspire awe, and we also know we can use them as functional tools; we can burn them to make fire and create shafts for arrows and spears. This story can be used to remind us of our connection with nature and our evolution.

Incorporating Myth into Our Magical Practice

Using the Daphne and Apollo story, I could write a spell using the transformation into a tree to visualize reconnecting with nature and the self. I could take Apollo's point of view and address a desire that is unsatisfied and meditate on how to solve it. I could even imagine Apollo having a conversation with Cupid where he apologizes for his insult, acknowledging the power of desire and that human emotions can be as powerful a force as an arrow. Human feeling and

human action are both strong—love and war. A ritual could be created using an actual arrow, breaking it to break a bond or heal from a broken relationship.

What else can we do? Individually, we must read and explore, and find what speaks to us on a personal level. Start with what you know. What myths were you raised with, if any? Do you have cultural or ethnic myths you can research? Find stories that resonate with you, not just personalities of deities. Seek out unfamiliar myths and make them meaningful to your life or a specific situation. That's what they're for. It's fine if they mean different things to different people, as long as they do have meaning. We can never know all the nuances a story had to the people of its time. We can only research, speculate, and then reinterpret the tales for ourselves.

Remember, storytellers were often seers—people who understood the boundaries of "other worlds." Learn the stories, read, examine artistic re-creations and expressions of the story, create a ritual, poem, spell, visualization—know the depth and various facets of the story. Read what experts say but also feel it for yourself and examine all the perspectives. Look for the shared human experiences and our relationship with nature. If we consider magic as a path to understanding our world and connecting with its energy, approaching myth in this way can lead us to an expanded awareness and acceptance of ourselves and our world, deepening our practice of magic.

BIBLIOGRAPHY

Campbell, Joseph. *Myths to Live By*. New York: Penguin Books, 1972.

———. *Pathways to Bliss: Mythology and Personal Transformation*. Novato, CA: New World Library, 2004.

Kane, Sean. *Wisdom of the Mythtellers*. Ontario: Broadview Press, 1994.

Leeming, David. *Myth: A Biography of Belief*. New York: Oxford University Press, 2002.

Morford, Mark, and Robert Lenardon, eds. *Classical Mythology*. 7th edition. New York: Oxford University Press, 2003.

Vandiver, Elizabeth, PhD. "Classical Mythology" (course no. 243). *The Great Courses*. Chantilly, VA: The Teaching Company, 2009.

Ember Grant *has been writing for the Llewellyn annuals since 2003. She is the author of two books,* Magical Candle Crafting *and* The Book of Crystal Spells. *Ember lives in Missouri and enjoys hiking, photography, and indulging in a variety of creative crafts. Visit her at embergrant.com.*

Illustrator: Rik Olson

The Lunar Calendar

September 2014 to December 2015

SEPTEMBER
S	M	T	W	T	F	S
	1	2	3	4	5	6
7	8	9	10	11	12	13
14	15	16	17	18	19	20
21	22	23	24	25	26	27
28	29	30				

OCTOBER
S	M	T	W	T	F	S
			1	2	3	4
5	6	7	8	9	10	11
12	13	14	15	16	17	18
19	20	21	22	23	24	25
26	27	28	29	30	31	

NOVEMBER
S	M	T	W	T	F	S
						1
2	3	4	5	6	7	8
9	10	11	12	13	14	15
16	17	18	19	20	21	22
23	24	25	26	27	28	29
30						

DECEMBER
S	M	T	W	T	F	S
	1	2	3	4	5	6
7	8	9	10	11	12	13
14	15	16	17	18	19	20
21	22	23	24	25	26	27
28	29	30	31			

2015

JANUARY
S	M	T	W	T	F	S
				1	2	3
4	5	6	7	8	9	10
11	12	13	14	15	16	17
18	19	20	21	22	23	24
25	26	27	28	29	30	31

FEBRUARY
S	M	T	W	T	F	S
1	2	3	4	5	6	7
8	9	10	11	12	13	14
15	16	17	18	19	20	21
22	23	24	25	26	27	28

MARCH
S	M	T	W	T	F	S
1	2	3	4	5	6	7
8	9	10	11	12	13	14
15	16	17	18	19	20	21
22	23	24	25	26	27	28
29	30	31				

APRIL
S	M	T	W	T	F	S
			1	2	3	4
5	6	7	8	9	10	11
12	13	14	15	16	17	18
19	20	21	22	23	24	25
26	27	28	29	30		

MAY
S	M	T	W	T	F	S
					1	2
3	4	5	6	7	8	9
10	11	12	13	14	15	16
17	18	19	20	21	22	23
24	25	26	27	28	29	30
31						

JUNE
S	M	T	W	T	F	S
	1	2	3	4	5	6
7	8	9	10	11	12	13
14	15	16	17	18	19	20
21	22	23	24	25	26	27
28	29	30				

JULY
S	M	T	W	T	F	S
			1	2	3	4
5	6	7	8	9	10	11
12	13	14	15	16	17	18
19	20	21	22	23	24	25
26	27	28	29	30	31	

AUGUST
S	M	T	W	T	F	S
						1
2	3	4	5	6	7	8
9	10	11	12	13	14	15
16	17	18	19	20	21	22
23	24	25	26	27	28	29
30	31					

SEPTEMBER
S	M	T	W	T	F	S
		1	2	3	4	5
6	7	8	9	10	11	12
13	14	15	16	17	18	19
20	21	22	23	24	25	26
27	28	29	30			

OCTOBER
S	M	T	W	T	F	S
				1	2	3
4	5	6	7	8	9	10
11	12	13	14	15	16	17
18	19	20	21	22	23	24
25	26	27	28	29	30	31

NOVEMBER
S	M	T	W	T	F	S
1	2	3	4	5	6	7
8	9	10	11	12	13	14
15	16	17	18	19	20	21
22	23	24	25	26	27	28
29	30					

DECEMBER
S	M	T	W	T	F	S
		1	2	3	4	5
6	7	8	9	10	11	12
13	14	15	16	17	18	19
20	21	22	23	24	25	26
27	28	29	30	31		

2014
SEPTEMBER

SU	M	TU	W	TH	F	SA
	1 Labor Day	2	3	4	5	6
7	8 ☺ Harvest Moon 9:38 pm	9	10	11	12	13
14	15	16	17	18	19	20
21	22 Mabon/ Fall Equinox	23	24 ● New Moon 2:14 am	25	26	27
28	29	30				

Times are in Eastern Time.

2014
OCTOBER

SU	M	TU	W	TH	F	SA
			1	2	3	4
5	6	7	8 ☺ Lunar Eclipse, Blood Moon 6:51 am	9	10	11
12	13 *Columbus Day* *(observed)*	14	15	16	17	18
19	20	21	22	23 ● Solar Eclipse, New Moon 5:57 pm	24	25
26	27	28	29	30	31 *Samhain/* *Halloween*	

Times are in Eastern Time.

2014
NOVEMBER

SU	M	TU	W	TH	F	SA
						1 *All Saints' Day*
2 *DST ends 2 am*	3	4 *Election Day* *(general)*	5	6　　☺ Mourning Moon, 5:23 pm	7	8
9	10	11 *Veterans Day*	12	13	14	15
16	17	18	19	20	21	22　　● New Moon 7:32 am
23	24	25	26	27 *Thanksgiving* *Day*	28	29
30						

Times are in Eastern Time.

2014
DECEMBER

SU	M	TU	W	TH	F	SA
	I	2	3	4	5	6 ☺ Long Nights Moon, 7:27 am
7	8	9	10	11	12	13
14	15	16	17	18	19	20
21 ● New Moon 8:36 pm Yule/ Winter Solstice	22	23	24 *Christmas Eve*	25 *Christmas Day*	26	27
28	29	30	31 *New Year's Eve*			

Times are in Eastern Time.

2015
JANUARY

SU	M	TU	W	TH	F	SA
				1 *New Year's Day*	2	3
4 ☺ Cold Moon 11:53 pm	5	6	7	8	9	10
11	12	13	14	15	16	17
18	19 *Martin Luther King, Jr. Day*	20 ● New Moon 8:14 am	21	22	23	24
25	26	27	28	29	30	31

Times are in Eastern Time.

2015
FEBRUARY

SU	M	TU	W	TH	F	SA
1	2	3 ☺	4	5	6	7
	Imbolc/ Groundhog Day	Quickening Moon, 6:09 pm				
8	9	10	11	12	13	14
15	16	17	18 ●	19	20	21
	Presidents' Day (observed)		New Moon 6:47 pm			
22	23	24	25	26	27	28

Times are in Eastern Time.

SU	M	TU	W	TH	F	SA
1	2	3	4	5 ☺ Storm Moon 1:05 pm	6	7
8 DST *begins 2 am*	9	10	11	12	13	14
15	16	17 St. Patrick's Day	18	19	20 ● Solar Eclipse, New Moon 5:36 am Ostara/ Spring Equinox	21
22	23	24	25	26	27	28
29	30	31				

Times are in Eastern Time.

2015
APRIL

SU	M	TU	W	TH	F	SA
			I All Fools' Day	2	3	4 ☺ Lunar Eclipse, Wind Moon 8:06 am
5	6	7	8	9	IO	II
I2	I3	I4	I5	I6	I7	I8 ● New Moon 2:57 pm
I9	20	2I	22 Earth Day	23	24	25
26	27	28	29	30		

Times are in Eastern Time.

2015
MAY

SU	M	TU	W	TH	F	SA
					1 *Beltane*	2
3 ☺ Flower Moon 11:42 pm	4	5	6	7	8	9
10	11 *Mother's Day*	12	13	14	15	16
17	18 ● New Moon 12:13 am	19	20	21	22	23
24	25 *Memorial Day (observed)*	26	27	28	29	30
31						

Times are in Eastern Time.

2015
JUNE

SU	M	TU	W	TH	F	SA
	1	2 ☺ Strong Sun Moon 12:19 pm	3	4	5	6
7	8	9	10	11	12	13
14 Flag Day	15	16 ● New Moon 10:05 am	17	18	19	20
21 Father's Day/ Litha/ Summer Solstice	22	23	24	25	26	27
28	29	30				

Times are in Eastern Time.

2015
JULY

SU	M	TU	W	TH	F	SA
			1 ☺ Blessing Moon 10:20 pm	2	3	4 *Independence Day*
5	6	7	8	9	10	11
12	13	14	15 ● New Moon 9:24 pm	16	17	18
19	20	21	22	23	24	25
26	27	28	29	30	31 ☺ Blue Moon 6:43 am	

Times are in Eastern Time.

2015
AUGUST

SU	M	TU	W	TH	F	SA
						1 *Lammas*
2	3	4	5	6	7	8
9	10	11	12	13	14 ● New Moon 10:53 am	15
16	17	18	19	20	21	22
23	24	25	26	27	28	29 ☺ Corn Moon 2:35 pm
30	31					

Times are in Eastern Time.

2015
SEPTEMBER

SU	M	TU	W	TH	F	SA
		1	2	3	4	5
6	7 *Labor Day*	8	9	10	11	12
13 ● Solar Eclipse, New Moon 2:41 am	14	15	16	17	18	19
20	21	22	23 *Mabon/ Fall Equinox*	24	25	26
27 ☺ Lunar Eclipse, Harvest Moon 10:51 pm	28	29	30			

Times are in Eastern Time.

2015
OCTOBER

SU	M	TU	W	TH	F	SA
				1	2	3
4	5	6	7	8	9	10
11	12 ● New Moon 8:06 pm *Columbus Day* *(observed)*	13	14	15	16	17
18	19	20	21	22	23	24
25	26	27 ☺ Blood Moon 8:05 am	28	29	30	31 *Samhain/* *Halloween*

Times are in Eastern Time.

2015
NOVEMBER

SU	M	TU	W	TH	F	SA
1 All Saints' Day/ DST ends 2 am	2	3 Election Day (general)	4	5	6	7
8	9	10	11 ● New Moon 12:47 pm Veterans Day	12	13	14
15	16	17	18	19	20	21
22	23	24	25 ☺ Mourning Moon, 5:44 pm	26 Thanksgiving Day	27	28
29	30					

Times are in Eastern Time.

2015
DECEMBER

SU	M	TU	W	TH	F	SA
		1	2	3	4	5
6	7	8	9	10	11 ● New Moon 5:29 am	12
13	14	15	16	17	18	19
20	21 Yule/ Winter Solstice	22	23	24 Christmas Eve	25 ☺ Long Nights Moon, 6:12 am Christmas Day	26
27	28	29	30	31 New Year's Eve		

Times are in Eastern Time.